Tough Pill
To Swallow

Annie Konovitch

Part of the Expanding Consciousness Series

First published by Dog Ear Publishing
4010 W. 86th Street, Ste H
Indianapolis, IN 46268
www.dogearpublishing.net

ISBN: 978-159858-437-0

This book is printed on acid-free paper.
This book is a work of Fiction. Places, events, and situations in this book
are purely Fictional and any resemblance to actual persons, living or dead,
is coincidental.

Printed in the United States of America

Dedication

To "Noah", "Centaury", "Gracie", "Eli", "Mama", and the extensive cast of additional characters in my life's book, who have mirrored back to me such a crystal clear image of myself.

Acknowledgments

I give special thanks to my love, Timmy, whose capacity, desire, and willingness to love me so deeply and passionately, grounds me and inspires me to pull in all of my energy and focus it on my highest expression.

I offer my humblest, deepest, sincerest thanks to my friend and sister, Concetta, my mom, and to Dog Ear Publishing for helping me with the painstaking editing process for this book. I am so grateful to them, and to all of my friends, for their ongoing support, guidance, encouragement, inspiration, and overall fabulousness on every level.

Part I

1

November 1998

He could tell by the unbridled excitement she was suppressing with a contorted face that she must have gotten the job: the job of a lifetime; the job she had done so well in school to get; the one she had researched and hunted for since before he knew her. It made all of her sacrifices worthwhile. She was there.

2

January 1999

It was a usual chilly, but not-so-cold, winter day in Southwest Florida. The typical infinite sunshine squished into a finite geographical location. Allie stared at the gray, choppy, winter water on either side of her. Rush hour was never fun and it always seemed to worsen right where she was, about halfway over the Howard Frankland Bridge heading towards Tampa. But she was supercharged with excitement over her intended destination–Tampa Airport. Traveling to Tampa Airport always carried with it so much promise for new, exciting adventures, and this one had the potential to be the biggest one yet. She carefully watched the signs as they came up. "Delta," she told the person driving. "Follow the blue."

She only had one suitcase and a garment bag. She brought these items to the curbside check-in and was greeted by a familiar face. She quickly glanced down at his identification tag to get his name again. When she saw it, she smiled to herself. How could she forget? Charlie Daniels. A mind movie started and she saw him hand her the boarding pass, then whip out a fiddle from behind the counter, and start dancing around playing "The Devil Went Down to Georgia". This was made even more amusing to her since she was going to Georgia. But she was no devil. His greeting stopped her movie and it was one of the many times when she was so glad humans weren't adept at mind reading yet. She left the counter with her boarding pass, for real this time, and couldn't help but be slightly disappointed about the lack of fanfare.

She entered the automatic glass door and her shoulder-length blonde hair was whooshed back by the blast of warmth that caused an intense temperature differential between the chilly outside and the heated terminal. She walked straight past the place where everybody was forming long, contained lines to check in. She could never understand why people did that. Just pay the customary dollar-per-bag tip at curbside check-in and be done with it!

As she made a right to get to the ascending escalator, she caught a glimpse of a cluster of hanging copper seagulls to her left. They looked so disarmingly beachy and friendly as they hung there, but she knew better. She heard their endless squawking every day and had been attacked and injured by one when she was a little girl on account of her eating a pot roast sandwich at the beach with her mom. Straight ahead she could see the metal tail feathers of better-favored coast dwellers, the pelicans. They were hanging from the ceiling in front of her, flying in the same direction she was walking, and she felt like she was one of the flock. She had always loved pelicans since she was eight years old when saw her first one on the dock of her grandparents' house. "You see that, Allie? That's a pelican," her mom told her. "Don't they look pre-historic?" She remembered that her mom went on to tell the history of the bird and she was fascinated. Her mom was always so knowledgeable about absolutely everything and it was cool, because she liked to learn and she had the best resource of all. It was like she had her very own Inter-net before it was even conceived of.

Although she hated to leave her flock, she returned to the present time and stepped onto the escalator heading to the terminal. She checked the boarding pass for the gate number and cross-referenced it on the screen at the top of the mechanical stairs. Terminal E. She headed to get the tram and suddenly became aware of the murmur of thousands of people floating into her ears. There were beautiful plants everywhere, and the shocking thing about them was that they were all real! *How did they do it?* she thought. They were perfectly kept–healthy, green and full. Tall palm trees of all different kinds, bushy peace lilies stretching up on top of metal posts with gold and sil-ver bowls holding philodendrons that reached down to the ground, and myriad bromeliads. The smell of differ-ent kinds of food wafted past her nose and the radio played, "No I can't go for that, I can't go for that..." until the standard loud airport messages and pages would cut in.

She stopped in the bathroom and there was a small line. She observed that, as usual, the bathroom was clean and well kept. She stared at the multi-colored mosaic on the walls with white tile as a backdrop, and knew that the patterns formed *something*. She concentrated, wanting to figure out what it was before it was her turn. "Ah," she gasped and then caught herself, remembering that not everyone was in on what she was thinking. They were waves–a flowing series of little blue waves with tiny gray crests.

She checked her hair as she was washing her hands and was alarmed to see the winter static was flaring up again. She used her wet hands to smooth down the random pieces and thought that it was a good thing she'd checked. She would only meet the new, local members of her training class once, and she didn't want their first impression of her to be of a young woman who had lived through a very recent electrocution.

She walked up to the tram and heard the mechanical male voice say, "We are about to depart..."

It was easy to spot the other new hires that were waiting to board the same plane as Allie. They were all clad in new suits and standing with nervous expectation. "Allie Kramer. Nice to meet you!" she all but squealed with an outstretched hand as the other local members of her new sales training class introduced themselves. It was a motley crew that boarded the plane to Atlanta that morning, but nothing compared to the total group of eighty-two characters that would convene to form the January 1999 Southeast Sales Training Class for one of the biggest pharmaceutical companies in the world.

After various hesitant niceties were exchanged, the imminent boarding began. Allie's stomach swarmed with the most massive congregation of butterflies she could ever remember. The mish-mosh of normal plane-boarding sounds were drowned out by the hurried outpouring of excited thoughts. As if her thoughts could come any faster than they usually did! The magnitude of this day was gaping in front of her like a twenty-thousand-foot cliff. Today meant permanent financial independence from her parents. It meant complete self-sufficiency. And most importantly, it meant the fulfillment of the Sagittarian ideal that was so much a part of her being–to help others.

3

ELLA MIONI PREPARED HER LAPTOP WITH LASER FOCUS. THIS wasn't her first PowerPoint presentation and God knows, it wouldn't be her last. In her short time at Millennium Pharmaceuticals she had attracted a lot of attention, not just for her striking good looks, but also for her dazzling stage performance. Every sales presentation she carefully constructed and performed was Oscar-worthy. Her presence was commanding and convincing. Not a single set of eyes would drift into boredom during her time in the spotlight. Her manager, Andrew Wells, had to fight the juicy temptation to smack her ass. He didn't know how much longer he could keep up his professional façade without blowing their cover on account of his overwhelming lust. But he never worried about *her* slipping up. She was incapable.

"Good Morning. I am Ella Mioni. I'm sure you all are just as excited as I am to be a part of something so much bigger than ourselves! This is the Sales Kitchen. You come in here as high quality raw ingredients, and will leave here fully prepared and transformed into a gourmet meal ; a meal your clients will want more of."

"On the overhead you'll see information I gathered from a book called *Spoiled*, written by Nicols Fox. You will also receive a copy of this passage. Always have it with you! This is why we are in business. Read it every day and on the days you feel tired or discouraged, read it twenty times. You are soldiers in the war against unsafe meat and the public health dangers that come with it.

She read aloud, "The conditions under which farm animals are raised presents all the conditions for infection and disease; the animals are closely confined; subjected to stress; often fed contaminated food and water; exposed to vectors (flies, mice, rats) that could carry contaminants from one flock to another; bedded on filth-collecting litter; every condition that predisposes the spread of disease from animal to human has actually worsened. Farming has become more intensive; slaughtering has become more mechanical and faster; products are processed in evermore massive lots and distribution has become wider..."

"Now, how does that make you all feel?"

Grace Avila, a young petite brunette, sighed, "Really glad to be selling livestock antibiotics." And she meant it. All of her feverish studies and life experience had brought her to this. The chance to make such a great impact on the food quality of the world and general public health made her shiver with gratitude.

Ella watched the mortified faces, feeling pleased with herself. It didn't matter to her that she had abbreviated the title and left out ten little words that changed the

whole meaning of the passage. Her job was to use emotion to incite passion in her sales force, and she was damn
good at it. What use did she have for the truth?

4

ALLIE WATCHED AS THE TROPICAL PARADISE SHE CALLED HOME dissolved into a field of cloud monsters. She didn't make forms out of the clouds this time. She was paralyzed with anticipation. She could hardly believe the materializing of her long-time dream: a job as a sales representative in the Human Health Division of Centaury Pharmaceuticals. Centaury was known for its safe, cutting-edge products, excellent training, benefits, and treatment of their employees, fair and conservative selling tactics, and humanitarianism. She thought proudly about the last two months. In November, she was still twenty-three. She remembered how her jaw dropped when she'd heard the details of her new job. A twenty-three-year-old making over forty-thousand dollars base pay; obscene health, dental, and retirement benefits; bonus potential of eleven-thousand dollars, maybe more; a company car, including car insurance; not to mention being shuttled on planes to great hotels for training; more food than she could ever eat; and yes, even dry-cleaning during the initial training phase of ten weeks. She shook her head as she thought of her parents trying to discourage her from leaving her job at the brokerage firm. How crazy was that? As she methodically buckled her seatbelt, the clicking seemed louder than it should have. She realized that was a mental alert she had programmed herself with. She was dwelling on the superficial again and it was time to pull out. She yanked herself out of the dazzle of the material realm, remembering that her primary concern was to help patients. She would now be responsible for educating doctors on the benefits and limitations of Centaury Pharmaceutical's products. She took this very seriously and wanted to be the best. She glanced over at a woman with what seemed to be her elderly mother, and smiled. Maybe her drugs would help *them*. She looked back out the window and swore she saw a cloud angel, she shifted her head, or maybe a turtle. She laughed at herself and tried to clear her mind.

5

I'M NOT VERY HANDSOME, HE THOUGHT WITH A FROWN. *Somebody will like me for who I really am, though. My mother likes me.* He was conscious of the dual nature of his feelings towards this concept. Yes, of course, his mother was his best friend and advocate. She was always there. Always. Actually, she really was there all of the time. She lived with him. Over time, he had come to figure out that the close relationship he had with his mother was definitely not healthy , but the guilt that consumed him every time he tried to put some distance between them wasn't worth it. When he was seventeen, he'd had offers for football scholarships to several major universities upon his graduation. It was precisely at the time when he had to pick which one he wanted to attend that his dear mother had a "heart spell" and fell ill. "The doctor said I have to take it easy for a while." Harvey was horrified. His mother had never been sick in his whole life, not even with a cold. He rushed around taking the best care of her possible in between school, practice, and games. He put off picking a school until his mother was back to normal. He really wanted to go to Notre Dame, because that's where his father went. His father had died when he was a baby. His mom said it was a drunk driver that ran into his car and killed him instantly. Harvey would always ask for more details about his life and death, but she would always tell him it didn't matter. "Some things were better left in the past," she would say. But he did, at least, know that he was smart, did well in school, loved playing football, and went to Notre Dame, all things that he chose to embody to the best of his ability.

As the deadlines for acceptance quickly approached, he panicked. His mother didn't seem to be getting any better at all. Not even a little bit. She knew that she controlled him through his guilt, so she felt very comfortable telling him, "I would absolutely hate it if my stupid spell got in the way of your dream. You have to go. Send in your acceptance while there's still time." The fact of the matter was that a big part of her desperately wanted for him to fulfill this dream, every dream, but the thought of having to be alone terrified her so much that she couldn't even consider it. Her parents had died young, her beloved husband even younger, and there was no way she could imagine, even for a second, that she would live without her baby boy.

The deadlines came and passed, and he tried to reassure himself that going to community college, and maybe never playing football again, wasn't really so bad. He didn't really have a choice. How could he leave his mother, who'd sacrificed all of her dreams to take care of him and raise him right? He would stay right there for as long as it took. So far, it had taken seventeen years. In two days, on January 21, he would be turning thirty-five years old. He felt like that age should *mean* something, like he should be doing great things, like he should be married and have a family. But he wasn't, and not only wasn't he, but he was really far away from it. He had never even been in a serious relationship. He hadn't actually been in *any* relationship.

For this birthday he felt like he had to do something, something that made a movement toward something greater. He sat watching people shovel the snow out of the walkways in front of their houses. He observed the unspoken shoveling protocol. Each person would shovel out the walkway one foot beyond their property line instead of stopping at the line. It was a neighborly thing to do, and Alexandria Bay was a neighborly little town. If you were the last one of the two neighbors on either side of you, you would have one foot less on each side to shovel. It was really a nice system. As he drank his coffee, he tried to figure out what this big birthday decision would be.

He had suspected for years that the magnitude of his mother's illness was not quite as great as she reported. He never did anything about it, paralyzed by his own half of the helplessly codependent situation. He looked outside and realized that he hadn't seen much, other than this view of the street, his whole life. He sat upright in his chair, an idea pushing through his thought and regret-infested brain. He would go to see her doctor.

6

GRACE AVILA PUSHED HER WAVY CHESTNUT HAIR AWAY FROM her face. Her emerald eyes held her trainer Ella Mioni with an idolized gaze. She loved to see a fellow spunky, smart, professional woman become so successful by looking out for the good of the world.

Andrew Wells leaned against the wall in the back of the training room with the same fixed gaze. He hung on her every word and was in awe of her every movement. He laughed, whispering to himself about her presentation, "She's really something else." Her convenient shortening of the title from which she cited her moving passage about farm conditions, *Spoiled: The Dangerous Truth about a Food Chain Gone Haywire*, to just *Spoiled*, was brilliant. And her way of leaving out just a few words from the quote, thereby changing the whole point the author was making, was nothing short of genius. This group wouldn't miss those few words, "and (the animals) were given antibiotics (which ironically made them more vulnerable to disease)." After all, they were getting paid a lot of money to sell antibiotics, not organic chickens.

7

"How is it okay that big pharmaceutical companies can buy votes?" Eli Tuntasit demanded of his father.

Tanti Tuntasit patted his son on the head. "Our resident conspiracy theorist is at it again!"

Eli pulled away with a furrowed brow. There's an implicit difference between theory and fact. Are you denying the facts?"

Tanti laughed good-heartedly. "My son, I am a scientist. I research and discover for the pure experience of discovery. I'm not interested in politics or legislation, or even finding cures. The pure process of discovery, creation, and recreation is exciting enough for me."

"Do you not care what becomes of your 'test-tube babies'?" Eli was pleased with himself. He'd coined this phrase for his father's discoveries, and would taunt him mercilessly with stories of what the "babies" could grow up to become.

"I thought votes were supposed to reflect the opinions and wishes of the masses, not the lucky few who could buy legislation with ridiculous amounts of money." Eli huffed in disgust and returned to the seat in front of his computer in his bedroom.

Tanti sat down with his coffee, shaking his head. The smile left his face. There had been a growing dissatisfaction in him for some time. He knew his son was right , but he wasn't ready to take responsibility for the possible damage his "babies" had caused, or still have yet to cause. The possibilities were too terrible to consider and anyway, once he made the discovery, its use, or potential misuse, was out of his hands. He was company property, as were his creations and discoveries.

8

As he walked into the small office that was in the front part of an old house, he felt it a really strange place to be starting his birthday. He was stepping into his mother's doctor's office, and it was for the absolute first time. How could that really be? All this time of taking care of her and he had never come, not even once, to see him. He knew the reason, but he marveled at the length of time that it had gone on.

His mother was a proud woman and although she was sick, she had two requests that she be allowed to control for herself: go to the doctor, and handle her medical tests and billing. She told him how hard it was for her to be so dependent on him, her only son. She had to be able to do something to maintain an inkling of independence. It seemed even more suspicious now than ever with the way that he was greeted after telling the receptionist who he was. Either she didn't have any bedside manner, or there was something strange going on. He figured that the office staff would have that look that is given when they ask how a patient is doing whom they know to be very ill. But there was no apologetic look. Nobody had the I-feel-so-sorry-for-you face. The receptionist directed him back to a small, well-lit room and there sat an aging but chipper man with a white coat. "Dr. Clarkson? I'm Harvey Akers, Stella Aker's son."

"Well, hello!" he responded, seeming a little surprised.

"I've come to talk about my mother's condition."

Dr. Clarkson sat up straight and furrowed his brow. "Condition?" he asked slowly.

The doctor hastily ushered him to the back with his hand as Harvey continued talking. "Yes, the condition that has kept me taking care of her for the last eighteen years?" he said, trying not to be patronizing, but feeling the beginning of what would be a lot of rage pouring out for a long time to come.

"Mr. Akers," the doctor spoke with perfect slow pronunciation, "your mother is in perfect health. She always has been, at least since I have known her, which is about eighteen years."

Harvey's heart rate quickened and his eyes started bulging.

"The way she has talked about you over this time made me think that she is a little codependent with you, which is to be expected after the things that happened in her life, but physically, she doesn't have a thing wrong with her."

A *little* codependent, Harvey thought without voicing it. *Yeah, I would say a little codependent!*

He was like a volcano getting ready to explode all over the old doctor and the entire small office. He got up quickly, not wanting to pull anyone else any further into this mess, thanked the doctor, and walked briskly out of the office.

Everything made sense! He'd always wondered why she insisted on traveling so far out of their town to see a new doctor. They'd had the same family doctor forever, and he lived right down the block. "I want to get a second opinion," she said. She had asked him to please honor her privacy and pride, and not talk to the family doctor or anyone else in town about her illness. He had honored it, not even thinking about how strange it all was.

He was boiling over with fury; he couldn't even get in his car. What else was she lying about? How much of his life had been a lie? He walked down the street. It was canopied with trees. He was breathing very fast, shallow breaths. He was having a nervous breakdown. His head was spinning. He fell into a bench and passed out.

He awoke to an old woman standing over him. "Are you okay, hunny?" she asked, gently prodding him with her cane.

"Uh, um," he stuttered, trying to get up.

"Better stay down there," she said, poking her cane into his stomach. "I'll get some help."

Even in his confusion, he could see that the woman was probably in need of more help getting around than he should be.

"Thank you so much, but I'm really fine." He thrust himself onto his feet before her reflexes could get the cane working again.

"I got some bad news and I just...well...I was just a little overwhelmed. But, I'm okay now. Thank you, again."

He ran off toward his car. For just a minute, he felt as light and free as a bird. No doubt there would be more anger to come, and plenty of healing to be done, but this news also meant he was free. He didn't have to stay managing the Dollar Store in downtown Alexandria Bay for the rest of his life. He didn't have to stay in the same small house that he grew up in, and had lived in his entire adult life until now. He could open himself to having hopes and dreams again, and for the first time, he had a real chance at having them fulfilled.

9

"GOOD GOD, IT'S LIKE THE ICE AGE OF 1999!" ALLIE reported to her mom from her hotel room in Atlanta, Georgia. Thirty-five degrees was about forty degrees lower than the low she was accustomed to.

"But, it's really cool to be here and I've met so many interesting people."

Allie's mom laughed at her unintentional pun. "Cool, huh?"

"Ma, come on!"

Allie hung up with her mom and looked at the room that was to be her home for nine more weeks. She still couldn't believe Centaury was paying for so many things for her. In class, one of her trainers told them that it cost well over a hundred thousand dollars for each new sales rep to be brought in, properly trained, and prepared for the "field". She laughed at the name they used to refer to the area the representatives worked in. *Moo*, she thought. Well, whatever they wanted to call it, she planned to make their investment worthwhile.

10

THIS TRAINING CLASS PROGRESSED LIKE ALL HE'D SEEN WITH Ella at the wheel–perfect, on course, and without any glitches. She mesmerized even the most passionate idealists in the class with her flawless fictitious personality. If they ever knew the devil she was, they would really be angry. It made him hot to think of it, and he looked at his watch for the third time in five minutes.

A knock came at the door and Andrew Wells opened it with his smooth charismatic smile. Ella walked in and handed him a pile of books and a bottle of wine, ignoring his expectant lips.

"There is nothing I like better than programming naïve optimists to be my moneymaking robots," she said with the devilish grin that was so yummy to Andrew. He couldn't wait anymore. He grabbed her from behind and pulled her small waist to him with both hands. She hid her reluctance and succumbed to his strong arms. Her disgust of him ran to the core, but her plan was right on track and she wouldn't have to deal with him much longer.

11

ELI PLOPPED DOWN ON THE CHAIR IN FRONT OF HIS computer. He was sick of being patted on the head and blatantly ignored. Why was he cursed with these circumstances? Being in constant contact with his zombified dad, who refused to think for himself, was getting on his last nerve and he couldn't wait for five more years so he could move out and get to the real work of changing the system. He had already started several on-line grassroots clubs to educate the masses of "drones". DBtH was his first idea. It stood for "Don't Believe the Hype". He started it as a club at school, but hesitant teachers squashed his group as soon as it started to get too much attention. He called them sissies and explained to them how they didn't have any balls. This ensured his suspension and brought Mrs. Tuntasit in for a very serious meeting with the principal. Kanta Tuntasit is her son's biggest supporter and a secret member of his on-line clubs , but she is careful how she handles public situations. She doesn't think the world has evolved to a point where people are ready for the wisdom behind his passion and precocious perspectives.

When confronted with questions regarding his extreme behavior, she explains that his crazy grandmother feeds him these outlandish ideas and encourages him to act out. Since she needs to be cared for in their home, she can't separate Eli from her, and it is a constant challenge. She shudders when she feels forced to lie. How could she ever explain if anyone ever found out what was *really* going on?

12

During the long drive home, Harvey tried to keep himself together as best he could. What would he say to his mother? What could he possibly say to her? Or should he even say anything?

This last question sparked a thought for a plan. He wouldn't say anything. Mother would be out at the library this afternoon and he would just leave. Just like that.

He regretted having to leave the owners of his store in the lurch, but he couldn't think too much about it. He had plenty of money saved after all this time, since he didn't really have any bills.

Now for his destination-he could go anywhere he wanted. He turned over volumes of pages in his mind that had been recorded from his life as an "armchair warrior". He had always wanted to go to New York City.

Growing up in upstate New York, he had always heard about stories of the big city. It was only hours away, but he had never gotten there. He thought there may be too much action downtown for his likes, but if he lived in the suburbs he could go downtown whenever he wanted and still maintain some semblance of the quiet life he was used to.

He wanted to finish school. He at least had his AA degree, but he wanted more. He loved learning. There would be so many schools to pick from when he got there.

As he approached his beloved home, he couldn't believe what he was planning. Just as he thought, the house was empty. He went up into the attic to look for a suitcase and found a light blue piece covered in dust. He dusted off as much as possible while still in the attic, and was blinded by the cloud and momentarily weak from sneezing. He worked quickly, but deliberately, to pack up his personal items and restore the house to the quiet, untouched look it usually had. When mother came home, she would find no clues as to the details of his disappearance, only a note.

"Dear Mother," he wrote staring coldly at the paper, "I have been in to see Dr. Clarkson today to check on the status of your condition. He informed me that there is no 'condition' and never has been. I am leaving so that I can try to make up for the years of life I have lost to your lies. Since you are perfectly healthy, you will not be needing my 'help' around the house. I lovingly suggest that you seek some help in the real areas that you need it: your mind. I will be doing the same in an attempt to undo the damage of the years of imprisonment your pain and fear have caused me. Please do not try to find me. I will be in touch when I am ready to deal with you."

He placed the salt and pepper shakers on either side of the top of the note and slipped out into the winter air.

13

THE LONG, TEDIOUS LECTURES, INTENSE STUDY SCHEDULE, and constant companionship of eighty-one other trainees were starting to wear on Allie's optimism. She missed her house, her boyfriend, her family, and most importantly, her life. She couldn't remember life before Centaury and that was beginning to weird her out. She began quietly consorting with her tablemates about cult theories. They were all starting to think that they were being watched and listened to a little too closely. The three of them would bust out of the hotel doors immediately after class and hold their tongues until they were clear across two streets. Then the excited chatter began. They talked over each other with reports of strange things they heard or saw. They seriously considered the idea that Centaury was a cult and that they were being subconsciously programmed. After some fresh air and some time of venting, they came to the conclusion that they were just delirious from stress, long days, and lack of sleep. They reminded each other that they were each strong independent thinkers, and that surely if they were being transmogrified by Centaury training, they would know, wouldn't they?

14

FINALLY HOME FOR THE NIGHT, ELLA MIONI GOT BACK TO her books. She would be damned if some fruitcake herbalists would rob her of her source of income and dream position: CEO of Millennium Pharmaceuticals. It was this perpetual spite that moved her to consistently find material for her classes in books that were written to take her industry down, or at least that's what she thought. Her festering anger wouldn't let through the notion that maybe people wrote books to educate other people, or to spark enough interest in them to do their own research and find their own truth. She took everything as a personal assault on her life and job, and revolted with the worst kind of rage. She kind of got off on turning their words against them. *What do we have here?* Her eyes ran through the highlighted boxes in Buhner's book *Herbal Antibiotics*:

"We have let our profligate use of antibiotics reshape the evolution of the microbial world and wrest any hope of safe management from us."

"Come on, give me something I can work with!" she said in disgust, continuing to read:

"Underestimating the evolutionary potential of living organisms is the single most important mistake made by those who use chemical means to subdue nature," she read with growing annoyance.

"One of the most important lessons from our ancient legend and myths is that the Gods take a dim view of human arrogance. An ancient version of this message is... found in the story of the woman who though she could weave better than the Gods and, after losing a weaving contest, was turned into a spider for her presumption." The master spinstress slammed the book down sure of one thing: she wouldn't lose this or any other contest. If the Gods wanted to test her, then she was ready.

15

ELI TUNTASIT RAN OUT OF SCHOOL. HE'D DONE A GOOD job of not getting suspended, per his mother's request, and in return was granted an extra half an hour twice a week with his favorite companion. He ran down the familiar street, his backpack bouncing behind him. He rounded the curve and crossed over into the park. There, on the bench under the shady elm, he found Emelda just where he'd left her. She looked up with wild eyes. "Hello, baby. Come here. Let's have a look at you! Now, this is the boy causing so much of a stir at his school," she said and smiled adoringly.

"But how did you *know?*"

She stopped him with her pointer finger outstretched over his lips. "Shh, Mama knows." He had known her as Mama since the first day they met. She slipped out once that her name was Emelda, and if he ever called her by name, he liked to use that.

"How'd your Mom take your suspension?" she asked slyly.

"Not too bad. She told me if I stay out of trouble, I can have more time with you before dinner."

"Good woman!" she exclaimed and smacked her leg in approval. "How are your memberships growing?" She was referring to his Internet organizations. One was DBtH, Don't Believe the Hype, which focused on what he called the "zombification" of Americans by the TV, newspapers, and magazines, and general unconscious living. The second one, STI, Stop The Ignorance, was broader in scope. It covered everything from shady political affiliations to environmental concerns.

"So far, so good," he replied without much excitement. "I posted a new website to my message board for STI this week. It's gotten a pretty good interest level."

"Something on the topic of the environment?" she asked with that look she always got when she knew something before he told her. Her knowledge levels on things were borderline supernatural. He wasn't much for flaky intuitive talk, but nothing in his regimented logical brain could explain her ways. So, intuition it must be. But he didn't like to get into that, and she knew it, which is why she always gave him that same taunting look. So, here it was again as she waited for his reply.

"*Yes*, it was an environmental topic. *Jeez*."

"Well, aren't you going to give me the details?" she playfully poked.

"Don't you already know?" he countered.

"Okay, okay, if you want to persist with this banter, leave my bench!"

His face softened and apologized for him. "You see, I typed in 'less junk mail' in a search engine and pulled up a website with a phone number to call, and an address to send a request to block the most popular sources of junk mail."

"Well, don't hold out on me," she teased.

She couldn't hold onto her laughter. Even he was doubled over. This was funny to them because Mama obviously couldn't receive junk mail at her park bench, which for a long time had been her only home.

16

Harvey settled in Elmhurst, New York, which was about ten miles out of the city. He took up residence on 77th Place, between Eliot Avenue and Caldwell Avenue. The choice of this location happened quite by accident. He had gotten off the highway to look for something to eat and wound up at a pizza place on Eliot Avenue. He overheard the thick New York accent of the Italian guy making the pizza. "My old lady is gonna kill me if I don't find someone to rent that apartment soon," he told his friend. Harvey's ears perked up. "Yeah, she wants to get seven-hundred dollars a month for it so she can go to beauty school."

"What the hell is beauty school?" his friend countered with the same thick accent. "She's already beautiful."

"Who knows? She says she wants to learn a trade, something she can get good at, and work in the city, and have some excitement."

"What's wrong with you? Aren't you exciting enough?" his friend cajoled.

Harvey interrupted the conversation. "I am interested in renting your apartment."

So, there he was. He liked it there. The Italian couple upstairs were nice and quiet, and Elmhurst had some of the small town feel that he was used to. All of the houses were connected and made of brick. There was an alley that ran behind the houses and this was how everyone got to their respective garages.

So much had happened in six weeks. His head was still spinning. He didn't know much, but he did know that he needed some help. He wanted so badly to bury the pain and betrayal, and never think of it and all of its implications again, but he knew that the result would be never having any peace or happiness. He decided to go out for a drive. He pulled out to Eliot Avenue and made a right. It wasn't long before he saw a church rise up on his left side. It was as if he could hear angels singing! The key to his healing, his salvation, would be there. He pulled into the parking lot and saw a sign that said: "Bible Study–Tuesday 7:00 p.m.". He grinned at his luck. It was 6:45 p.m. on Tuesday. He reveled in the comfort of the synchronicity, and for a moment he felt sure everything was going to be all right.

17

Five weeks down, five weeks to go. Allie looked out of the window of the hotel room that had become her cell. Clawing her way back to her eternally optimistic disposition was hard this morning. She was cold, tired, and if she had to eat any more crap or sit in that room all day for one more day, she would lose it for sure. She got a hold of her emotions and began reminding herself of all the amazingly positive aspects of her circumstances. Although five or six people had dropped out of her training class, there were still at least seventy-five really cool, smart, interesting people that she was lucky enough to get to know. They were teachers, nurses, and other sales representatives from the same and different fields, all from different Southeastern states, different cultures and life experiences. Training was halfway over and she just knew that when she got home and into the normal routine of her job, she would love it. The information she had learned about her drugs compared to competitors had given her the confidence to stop worrying about being programmed into a cult member. Centaury had been continually stressing the importance of feeling "ownership" for the drugs that each rep was to sell. At first that had felt like a big part of her "cult" concern, but now she liked it. She felt comfortable feeling like the drugs she was to sell were hers, too. It seemed clear from all the studies she'd looked at that her drugs were far superior. She would soon be translating that information out into the field where it could be of life-changing use to the thousands of patients she would indirectly affect through doctor education. Things really weren't so bad. She took a deep breath, grabbed her sweater, and headed down to her usual table.

18

THE ORLANDO WORLD CENTER MARRIOTT RESORT welcomed Ella Mioni with all of its grandeur. It was a monstrosity of a complex complete with ten restaurants and lounges, golf course, impressive pool, world-class spa, and everything else imaginable. She wasn't much for idle time, so all of these resort options existed on a different plane from her. She marched in and up to her training room where her Eastern Sales Team waited patiently. Ella was never late, but her temperament demanded that everyone be there even before she was, and they knew it.

Grace Avila carefully organized her notes and books. She was always prepared. Her small hand wrote the date neatly in the right-hand corner of her notebook: March 1, 1999. This was the last week of her training. Next week she would start in her new territory: the whole State of Florida. She wasn't daunted by the driving time. She wasn't daunted by anything. She had only one drug to focus on representing: Pylobact, a flouroquinolone antibiotic for use in chickens and turkeys. *It's very easy to administer. Just add it to their water,* she thought to herself smiling. Ella's phrases always stuck in their brains. They would joke that she sent an Ella doll with them when they left class for the day and each button would access a different phrase:

"Animals that are administered antibiotics gain four to five percent more body weight than those who do not receive antibiotics."

"You are soldiers in the war against unsafe meat and the public health dangers that come with it!"

"A Pylobact chicken is a safe chicken."

Ella started class and Grace snapped back into the moment.

"Okay, let's see who is prepared today."

Grace shifted in her seat preparing to raise her arm at any second.

"What percentage of chickens and turkeys are infected with Campylobacter?"

She barely got the question out and Grace's hand flew up.

"Yes, Ms. Avila."

"Seventy-ninety percent."

"Excellent."

"Seventy-ninety percent of chickens and turkeys are infected with Campylobacter," Grace laughed to herself. She could tell this was going to be another phrase for the Ella doll.

"Okay, so I hate to have to state the obvious, but why is this important to our purpose?"

Grace shot her hand up like a rocket and started answering without being called. "Because that means every farmer who raises livestock needs our drug."

"Very good, Grace."

Every farmer... The words hung over them like a thick Pacific fog.

19

Mrs. Tuntasit was making the last dinner preparations when Eli came in.

"Just on time," she beamed.

Tanti hadn't come home just yet.

"Your father should be here any second. Are you hungry?"

"Yes, Ma'am!"

"How was your visit with Mama?" She always laughed at this name Emelda called herself.

"Good. She gave me a new assignment."

"Do you want to talk about it?"

"Not just yet. Let me see what I find out first."

She continued to bustle around the kitchen musing over just how strange the situation really was. She would forget sometimes, because it was so familiar to them. Mama was really the "crazy grandmother" that supposedly lived with them, and Kanta actually encouraged Eli to spend time with her! If her husband knew, she was sure he would commit them both. But she'd seen so much growth in Eli during his talks and assignments with her that she couldn't help but be supportive. It had been going on for about six months, since the beginning of the school year. He passed her bench every day going to and from school, and she was always there. But something happened that one day in September and he said hello to her. Kanta had taught her son to balance being polite and respectful with being street-smart. Living in the close-range Philadelphia suburbs had its dangers. When he greeted her that day, she said, "Sit down, boy. What took you so long?"

Eli hurried to his room to sneak in some research time before his dad got home and dinner started. He thrived on his assignments from Mama. It had been information that he gathered through previous homework from her that spurred him to start his public action groups. She never told him what to do or how best to use his time. She wanted to empower him by piquing his interest enough to want to look for more information to find what felt true for him. The assignments came as a result of his interest in the topics they discussed. He always asked how best he could find out more, and so the assignments were born.

He quickly typed "campaign contributions pharmaceutical companies" into the search engine. The words flowed out easily, since he was no stranger to this type of search. She suggested he start there because it was familiar territory. From there she suggested a slight tweak that intrigued him. What he saw made him sick. "My God," he said out loud, and it felt like his stomach dropped ten stories.

20

Harvey looked shyly around the classroom. It was open and the light was on, but it was empty. He was so glad that he was the first one there. Nothing was more frightening to him than walking in a room full of people. Even if none of them were looking at him walk in, he felt like they all were, and it set his nerves into the worst kind of frazzle.

He eyeballed the chairs, which were plastic with metal legs, and chose one as far away from everything as possible. He sat down and almost immediately he heard footsteps moving down the hall. As he listened, he was strangely intrigued. They were so light-sounding that he could barely believe they were human. When the door opened, he understood...it was an angel.

Paula Markinson introduced herself quickly and politely, but Harvey was too stunned to answer. He was in love with this woman and his voice box was instantly paralyzed. Her eyes were a magnificent shade of light blue and her gleaming brown hair fell on her face in soft curls. Her delicate white hands were holding a notebook and a bible. Eventually, Harvey was able to eke out a "hello" and an introduction. She asked him if he was new to the church and he fumbled out some gravely succinct explanation of his move. He couldn't get over her softness. Everything looked so soft! It was such a stark contrast compared to his mother, who was the only woman he'd spent any real amount of time with.

The awkwardness was finally broken with the entrance of a group of three women and a man.

Harvey tried to hide his staring, but he was in awe of her beauty. He looked at her sadly, thinking for sure she was taken and if she wasn't, she definitely would never be interested in him.

Class officially started when an older man, who introduced himself as Reverend Sam, entered the room and closed the door.

Reverend Sam was really a progressive minister when you consider the fact that he was a member of a Catholic Church. His style of bible teaching was unconventional, but his sermons and classes were always well attended, so they gave him free reign. He started to smile and began speaking. "Keep your bibles closed today; we won't be using them. Does everybody have paper?" he asked, glancing around the room and placing small piles of blank paper at the end of each of the tables. He continued, "Our capacity to love God and each other, dramatically increases the more we can love ourselves. The more whole and complete we are inside, the better we can wholly and completely love others and Him. So, our work cannot just be with kind acts. We must face our demons, bravely and diligently, for it is only when we clear them out that we can clearly see God's face in our own. Today is the day we start to look inside."

Harvey smiled on the inside, knowing that his luck was more than just random. Not only did he meet the woman that he wanted to marry, at the same time he was given the tools to try to make himself good enough for her.

"God's Oneness and the Kingdom of Heaven lie in a place above and beyond the separation of the human mind. Duality is intrinsic in our experience on this Earth, because of the duality of the human mind. Left hemisphere and right hemisphere–two separate parts of us that control us. Conscious mind and unconscious mind–more separation that leads to the human experience of separation. But the good news is that although we are in human form, we are spirit, and we are not locked into the experience of separation. It is only by unifying the opposites in the mind that we unify the opposites in our experience, and return to the oneness beyond them. We can experience Heaven on Earth. It is a state of mind."

As Reverend Sam stopped talking for a moment, there were varying degrees of discomfort rising in the room. Heaven on Earth...Heaven is a state of mind? Was that in the bible?

Although the discomfort was obvious, no one spoke. Reverend Sam continued, "And reaching the state of mind that is Heaven is easy when you know how. Now, I want each of you to take the next half hour and write a story explaining something that has been causing you grief or distress of any kind. Be as elaborate and detailed as possible with your descriptions of things. If you get stuck or need some support while the emotions are coming up, I'll be right here."

Everybody followed the instructions without speaking. Harvey shifted around in his seat wondering for a second if he should have come, but then immediately knowing that this was the nature of the beast. There is always resistance to looking inside. That is why people do everything they can to avoid it. He looked over at Pam and his eyes flashed with determination. He picked up his pen, took a deep breath, and took the plunge into the tragic story of his life.

21

Allie hit the ground running with her clean, organized sales binder, new suits and tenacious personality. The several months that followed her "release" from training were a blur. She couldn't believe it was already June, the time they had all been waiting for. Such a momentous time in history and she was a big part of it: the launch of Centaury's Superdrug that would change the scope of traditional Non-Steroidal Anti-Inflammatory Drug use. She was so excited she had chills, despite the disgusting, hot, humid, weather that claimed at least five to six full months of the Florida year. She was packed and ready to go to San Francisco for the long-awaited Senecox Launch Meeting. It was her first time to the West Coast and the anticipation was overwhelming. She would see the Golden Gate Bridge, Elephant seals, and more Ghirardelli chocolate than in her wildest dreams. With the very thought of chocolate, her thoughts switched to her dear friend that she had barely talked to over the last six months. They had both started new, exciting jobs and were so focused on them that they slipped up on their habitual phone connection a little more than either would like. *I will bring her back mass quantities of chocolate,* she thought as her face brightened. She fell into the pages of memories they shared. They had met in Spain during college and had been the closest friends ever since. They were planning a trip to Vermont in the fall, but they had to wait until it was closer to solidify the plans. They were both officially slaves to their planners and their jobs now. She finally decided she had to call her to catch up before she left. She dialed the phone number so fast that she didn't even need to consult her cell phone's address book. Her eyes all but welled up when it clicked directly to voice mail. "Damn it," she pouted. The message tone beeped and she said, "Gracie, it's me. I miss you and I can't wait to catch up. I'm leaving now for San Francisco for the Senecox Launch Meeting and my phone doesn't work there. I hope all is well. Call me soon."

22

GRACE AVILA TRUDGED UP THE STAIRS TO HER APARTMENT. It had been a long day. She'd had field visits with her manager two days in a row and she was over it. When she left training in March, she was disappointed to not see Ella Mioni anymore. She so admired her. A friend in the field had cautioned her, "You'll be surprised to see where people pop up in pharmaceutical companies. One day they're your trainer, the next your boss." Boy, she was right on. That is precisely what happened. In May, Ella had been promoted from Sales Trainer to ESM–Eastern Seaboard Manager. That was another thing her friend had told her about: the acronyms, acronyms for everything. It was like a different language that could only be understood by people on the inside–kind of like a cult. Grace was so happy to have Ella back, at first. But by now she was starting to get this weird vibe from her. She couldn't quite put her finger on it. Besides that, she was working her like a dog.

She sat down and shifted into her night job; no time for rest. She opened her laptop and while it was warming up, started to listen to her cell phone messages. When she was done with that, she had to clear and deal with all of the messages on her Millennium voicemail system. Then she would check her e-mails, do her expense reports, and fill out the mountain of new spreadsheets Ella created to torture her with. She was starting to be really sure that Ella stayed up late thinking of ways to wield her power over others, and just generally piss people off.

She rolled her eyes at the barrage of stupid messages with "time-sensitive" things that clients needed. She wanted to kick herself in the ass for ever being so eager to help that she plastered her cell number all over her business cards. She wouldn't do that anymore, but the damage had already been done. She scoffed at, and skipped, the ones she couldn't handle right now and came to the last one. It was a familiar voice— Allie. She looked at the time and realized she was already on the plane and would be without her phone. She hung up the phone and prayed out loud, "Please God, tell her I need to talk so she'll call me from the hotel."

23

Eli stared at the screen in disbelief. His skin was as white as his walls and he felt dizzy. How could he be so blind? How could he be so ignorant? He had been so focused on revamping the crooked health care system that he completely missed the fact that it was really the entire U.S. government, from the township level up to the federal level, that needed to be completely reworked. His head swirled with the immensity of the job at hand. How were a thirteen-year-old boy and a sixty-four-year-old homeless woman going to fix this?

His eyes were frozen on the screen in front of him:
Campaign contributions-
Wall Street 23.2 million
Telecommunications 14.4 million
Oil and Gas 14.3 million
Banks 11.5 million
Pharmaceutical Companies 8.3 million
Accountants 6.9 million
Hollywood 6.5 million
Big Tobacco 6.1 million
Computers 5 million

Alcohol 4.9 million
Gambling Casinos 4.1 million
Defense Contractors 4 million
Airlines 3 million
Health Care 2.1 million
Industry titans-
Founder of Amway 1 million +
Chiquita Brands International 536,000

Eli blinked and looked at the computer again. All of these special interests groups were using their financial influence to get legislation passed without the people of the country being educated and involved in the process. The situation was graver than he could comprehend.

"Eli, dinner!" Kanta Tuntasit shouted.

24

EVEN THOUGH THE EXERCISES REVEREND SAM WAS HAVING them do seemed very strange for a bible study class, everyone continued without question, having the faith and the knowing that he was on to something. After they each wrote their story, the Reverend had them circle the phrases and words that carried a lot of emotional charge for them. Then they were to write all of the charged words and phrases in a column on the left of the paper. Next, he directed them to take as much time as needed to figure out the opposite of each word and phrase. Some words and phrases could have more than one opposite. This part of the exercise carried them through the end of the class and they were encouraged to take home their respective lists and continue to work on the opposites. When they returned to class next time, they would each do a prayer offering up the imbalanced states of mind to God and giving thanks for the freedom from the pendulum swing back and forth between the opposites.

Harvey left class intending to do his homework knowing it would be the start of the process that would completely change his life.

25

WITH EYES CLOSED, ALLIE SAT AT THE WHARF OVERLOOKING San Francisco Bay. She wanted to soak in every inch of this amazing place and every moment of the perfect weather. California in June was surely one of life's greatest pleasures. Her meetings started Monday and she'd come early to have some tourist time. She had used her time well: Chinatown, Sausalito, and Muir Woods. She returned to her hotel and mentally prepared for the week. It sure was nice to have a free trip to San Francisco.

Monday morning came too quickly and Allie let the wave of sales reps, who were all heading towards the opening presentation, carry her along like a plastic bottle in the ocean. They each scrambled to a seat while Hip-Hop music blasted and foam balls were thrown around. The excitement was contagious. Allie was sure this was the point that the event coordinators were trying to get across. They pass the energy to us, we pass it to our doctors, they pass it to their patients, who pass it to their pharmacists by filling prescriptions, and the script numbers get passed back to corporate and on to the investors and Wall Street. Nice set-up.

Sandy France had a magnetic presence. Everybody loved her. Sandy was the Southeast Sales Director and she was great. Everyone was thoroughly pumped up about Centaury's new Superdrug. It would help millions, maybe even billions, of people have a better quality of life and possibly save them from a gastrointestinal ulcer, perforation, or bleed. It could even save their lives. Allie felt like she, and everyone else, there were really ready to launch this drug.

Allie pushed through the long meetings, which had full breakfast and lunch buffets and break spreads with chocolate-covered strawberries and make-your-own-sundae stations. The week was going so fast. She was mindful for what seemed like the thousandth time of how grateful she was for her raging metabolism that allowed her to eat like a maniac and not gain weight. She watched many reps staring longingly at the goodies and then deciding to grab a banana in disgust.

Allie sat in her room and put her feet up. She noticed a small ice cream stain on her blouse. Shaking her head at her animalistic eating habits, she pulled the company-paid calling card out of her purse. It was time to check in with the small part of a life she still had.

26

THE SOUND OF THE CELL PHONE STARTLED HER. SHE PUT THE pint of Ben & Jerry's Chubby Hubby on the coffee table and stuck the spoon in the top. She had just started eating and it was still frozen enough to stick straight up like a monument to the healing powers of the ice cream Gods. She scrambled for the phone and answered it just in time.

"Gracie?" she heard when she answered.

"Oh my gosh, Allie! You got my telepathic message!"

"Of course!" was the familiar response. They were always on the same page.

"Are you still in San Francisco?"

"Yeah, I leave Friday. But, never mind me, how are *you?*"

"Sweet Jesus! How much time do you have?"

Allie giggled, "As long as it takes."

"Okay, well here goes...I'm stressed, I'm tired, my manager is a tyrant bitch, I drive so much that when I finally stop driving, I go to sleep and I *dream* that I'm driving, and if I have to talk about another freakin' chicken or turkey, I will snap for sure."

"Wow! Okay."

"What about you?"

"Better than you are right now."

"Allie," she said and the tears started flowing, "it's just not what I thought it would be. I got into this to help increase the quality of health, but I didn't realize it would be such a detriment to my own well-being. Nobody cares about how good my product is, just how cheap it is, because the huge meat companies own all the farmers. I feel beaten down, alone and I don't know what's right anymore. I heard something on the news about Superbugs that were forming because of too much antibiotic use. What if that's true? What if I'm the problem? What if I'm public health enemy number one instead of one of the 'soldiers of health' my trainer/new boss calls us?"

27

THE WHIRLWIND OF THE SENECOX LAUNCH WAS STILL unfolding. It had been six months of early mornings, long days, night programs and full working weekends. The pharmaceutical industry was such a different world than anything Allie had imagined. Now it was her world. She ate at the best restaurants and became a connoisseur of wines and ports. The goal was to educate the prescribers. This education would naturally result in doctors writing her drugs because the science spoke for itself, right? All for the purpose of the best choice for the patient–that was the original point. Then, how had she been catapulted into an alternative universe where scripts could be bought, competitors would habitually steal samples, and patients were seen by the doctor for five minutes, tops? Allie had a breakdown. What had happened to her perfect world? She asked her boyfriend of almost four years to move out, stopped sharing the flowing wine at night programs, and tried to rebuild her life. She knew there had to be something better than this as her contribution to humanity. She reflected over the eight months of being in doctors' offices every day, all day. What did she see? Waiting rooms full of people, all ages, but mostly senior citizens (given her territory of Clearwater up through New Port Richey) who would wait sometimes hours to be seen for minutes, carrying bags full of medications that they didn't know by name, or what they were even taking them for, and they weren't getting any better. Some of them would make snide comments to each other loud enough so Allie could hear them, about the price of drugs and the crooked bastards who ran the drug companies, and then glare at her shamelessly. Maybe they were right. She always had the canned answer to any of these comments available in case anyone directly confronted her about them, but the answers weren't making sense anymore. The insurance companies wouldn't pay for preventative drugs, even though they cost less than the incidences they were formulated to prevent.

She decided to become a student of her circumstances. "What could I learn in this environment that I could use to help change it?" she pondered. She started to read books she had never touched before; books about the human spirit, spirituality, and self-improvement; books about the synchronicities in life. That's when she discovered that she was exactly where she was supposed to be. So, she continued on the quest to gather information to better serve the world all under the guise of a pharmaceutical rep. By this time she had mastered the use of her internal crap filter to siphon out the things in her job that were really time-sensitive from the one-hundred daily "urgent" e-mails and voice mails. She went on this path of self-discovery, spiritual discovery and industry discovery for seven months, and then something amazing happened. She fell in love.

Part II

1

THE NEW ELEMENT OF LOVE IN HER LIFE, AND THE WAY IT came about, hit Allie really hard. All the spiritual goals that she had been bringing into focus were suddenly brought to an even higher level.

It was the Memorial Day Weekend of 2000. At the last minute, Allie had decided to accept an invitation to accompany some friends to Key West. At this point, almost all of the people she hung out with were people that she'd met through Centaury. She had been told by one of the members of her sales cluster on her first day that before she knew it, her whole world would be Centaury. All of her friends would be from Centaury. All of her time would be spent doing Centaury-related things. She wasn't kidding. But, it wasn't a bad situation in the friend department, because the friends she had acquired were so fun, interesting, and spectacular, and were genuinely good people.

So, they were off to the southernmost point of the United States. The excitement was overwhelming. Allie had never been to Key West and she had never been on a co-ed friend trip of this nature as a single adult. The freedom and fun was exhilarating. They had a really cool townhouse in Truman Annex and experienced the best fun Key West had to offer. They went fishing, ate their own catch, drank, danced, and shopped. They napped, sang, and roamed the streets. They went to Mallory Square for its daily Sunset Celebration, and it was there that Allie spoke to her first psychic. The psychic, without having been given any information, tapped into the growing spiritual focus Allie had been experiencing. Among other things, she had told Allie to mentally draw a five-pointed star of light around herself every day and night. She made special mention of the graveyard there in town. She explained that five planes of electromagnetic energy cross over it in such a way that doesn't exist anywhere else in the world. She encouraged Allie to go experience "the energy" while she was there. The crew she came with wasn't really the graveyard-going type, so she laughed off that idea and continued on the wild adventure.

It was their last night and as they were gearing up for the final night festivities at Fat Tuesday's on Duval Street, Allie saw a familiar face.

"Holy shit, is that Noah? It can't be."

Well, it could be and it was. Noah was a very strange blast from the past. Noah was good friends with John, the boyfriend that Allie had dated for almost four years and had asked to leave seven months before. She and John had actually rented a room in Noah's house and were his roommates for four months at the beginning of their relationship. The relationship that Allie had with Noah was antagonistic at best, and seeing him brought up some of the unresolved weirdness. Somehow, she didn't remember him being so good-looking. How had she lived in the same house with him for four months and never noticed?

She came down the few steps to the sidewalk and he looked up at her from a swarm of long, blondish hair. His eyes were alarmingly deep and piercingly blue. Complexity spilled from them like a waterfall. She was disgusted and intrigued. He had his usual aloof demeanor and their greetings ended quickly. Allie's mind was reeling with this strange coincidence. She finally got over it and went on with the nighttime activities.

She and the crew were parked at the bar at Rick's. It seemed like just as soon as he was out of her mind, he came walking into the bar. The music was eardrum blasting and bodies flung themselves everywhere under the guise of dancing. Allie and Noah were pulled together through the noise and crowd in a way that would have to suggest divine intervention. They moved together with intensity and curiosity. She felt like time had stopped. After who knows how long, when his friends were leaving, Noah wrote his phone number on the back of Allie's plastic brush and asked her to call him in the morning so that he could take her and her friends out on his boat. She said that they were leaving to go home in the morning, but that she would call some other time to say "hi". He left and she thoughtfully put the brush back in her straw bag. She no sooner looked back up and he was standing in front of her again. His friends had already left and with them went his obligations to them. Their eyes locked, but they broke the connection knowing it was too soon to kiss. It was too soon for anything really. They were both so overwhelmed with the intensity and strangeness of the whole thing.

2

Spring in the suburbs of Philadelphia was always worth waiting for through the crappy winter. By June the snow had long melted away, and the downtown streets and parks erupted with colors and scents. Eli passed an overgrown thicket of rugosa roses. Strong fragrance wafted out of their crinkly, pink bunches. He admired the long, thin, thready leaves of a cluster of Siberian irises and mused on the color of the flower. It could best be described as cobalt blue, but with less blue and more purple. He smirked as he thought, *At least they haven't killed these off yet.* He tried not to let this pang of anti-government anger ruin the perfect spring day. The shock of the complexity of the problems with the governmental and social structures of the country had not worn off yet. As he walked briskly, Eli mulled over the past year. He had spent the better part of the year doing research, reading everything he could to educate himself on every topic possible to prepare him for the feat ahead of him—to come up with a new governmental and social structure for the United States. He wanted to start with the health care system and then flow over into politics as it related to that field, and then move on to the rest of the issues from there. He was still very far away from any solid form, but he did have notebooks of notes he had taken through his continuous research. He realized that the only way to begin to make the necessary changes was to first figure out what had happened to bring the system to its current state.

During the last year he hadn't seen Mama as regularly as before. He wanted to use as much of his free time as possible to throw himself into the research process. Emelda encouraged him along the way, but she didn't give him much to go on. He always felt like she knew the answer to the country's and maybe even the world's, problems, but wasn't letting him in on it. Whenever he would accuse her, she would laugh and smack her leg in the familiar fashion, and say, "Oh hunny! Do us all a favor and convert your paranoia to energy for problem solving. Do you want to fix this mess or blanket Mama with accusations!?" Her way was so disarming that he couldn't stay mad at her. He would roll his eyes and shake his head in disapproval, and then get back to business.

In the last year, the hits to his websites had more than tripled. He was constantly supplying the increasing number of visitors with information he deemed worthwhile. As he educated himself, he passed along his discoveries to his reader base. He was still working out his web entries for tonight after school when he arrived at Mama's bench.

"Well, hello stranger!" she chuckled with that same laugh that always seemed to defy her apparent circumstances. Eli plopped his knapsack down on the ground and took the empty seat next to her. Neither of them were big fans of small talk, so it didn't take long for them to get into good conversation. It didn't matter how much time had passed, they would always pick up as if it were the day before that they had seen each other.

"So, what are you working on today?" Mama asked with excitement.

"Well, I've been looking over my notes from a book I read called *The Social Transformation of American Medicine*, by Paul Starr. In the book, he gives a chronological account of the influences that he believes came together to create the current inextricable ties between health care, government, money, and power. He talks about a time when doctors were not part of the upper echelons of society, but rather part of the normal society. Most healing was done at home and usually came from the mother in the family, and a doctor was only called in when there was nothing in the home arsenal to help the illness. Doctors were respected and trusted, but were not paid well. This seems to me like a noteworthy point: people were attracted to the health care field for the right reasons, not for money or power. He went on to explain that during that time, which was the mid to late eighteen hundreds, there was a movement led by some doctors to make the field more exclusive. "They appealed to the universities to try to restrict the membership and practice of physicians. They started to speak against lay healers that they didn't feel were properly educated. At the same time, the pharmaceutical industry was at its beginning and for the first time health was linked to profit, a cycle that has perpetuated ever since."

"Well, it sounds like you've been doing your homework! How do you feel about what you've uncovered?"

"I have a little better understanding of the cause and effect of the culmination of historical events leading up to now, but I don't feel any closer to a resolution than I did a year ago," he said as he winced with the thought of his fruitless labor.

"Consider extending the range of your reading to include the works of the great philosophers. The regimented nature of the social and governmental history, and analysis you're pursuing, is keeping you in a box. It is the same box that everyone else has been in throughout the time it has taken to get our country to its current state."

Eli glazed over. He always associated philosophy with lack of outcome. He didn't see any point of dreamily observing all the problems without using that information to make a difference.

Mama laughed and alternated her leg slapping with some foot stamping. She used this combo when she was especially tickled about something, "I know, you don't see any point!"

Mama's eyes glittered with the gift of clear sight. Eli didn't even realize that *he* was a philosopher!

3

GRACE WAS DRIVING THROUGH AN EXCEPTIONALLY BEAUTIFUL part of her sales territory in North Florida. Huge, old, live oaks canopied the street and cow pastures with rolling stretches of green extended further out than the eye could see. She was blasting her favorite classical music and feeling content. She was worlds away from the confusion and concerns of a year ago. Ella had gotten promoted again, which put her out of any contact with Grace; there was a territory restructuring done, which cut her work area in half; and her faith in her products and her perception of her place in the world was restored. She loved her counterparts and her salary. She was in the top ranking of her sales team on account of her deep passion for her work. Life was good.

She pulled in to a little diner. She didn't pack lunch today. She greeted the waitress with a brilliant smile. "Just one, please."

The woman swung her wide hips around an old wood podium in order to grab a menu, barely making it out of the tight quarters without knocking the structure down altogether. "Right this way, sweetie!" she said with a thick accent that gave away her southern roots. She tucked a wiry, grayish, strand of hair back into her tight bun and swung her hips through the aisle, narrowly missing chairs, arms, and anything else that made the mistake of being in her path.

Grace walked with her eyes glued on the sight in front of her. *God*, she thought, *I hope my hips don't ever look like that!* She chuckled to herself as she created a comic strip in her mind of a character called Hurricane Hips. The hips had a mind of their own; they were seriously like their own separate entity. The comical fantasy ended in an instant when they reached a booth at the end of the aisle next to the window. Grace thanked her politely then, when she had turned her back, wiped one side of the booth off with a napkin. She wanted to make very sure that her new, pink, silk, Ann Taylor suit would make it through her lunch excursion unscathed. Her territory was beautiful, but given its rural nature was full of establishments that were not up to her cleanliness standards.

She noticed someone had left a newspaper at the table and began to open it when the same waitress returned to see what she wanted to drink. She thought, *Chardonnay, please*, but said, "Do you have bottled water?"

"No sorry, just Florida's finest!" she replied, thinking how it was funny that city folk were all the same.

"Just a decaf coffee then," Grace said, thinking about how she longed to be in more classy surroundings.

"You got it," the waitress said, thinking, *What did she think the coffee was made out of!?*

Grace glossed over the articles. The waitress returned with her water in a chipped and cracked, red plastic Coca-Cola glass. Grace reluctantly ordered a turkey sandwich. She hoped the restaurant got their turkey from close by, then at least she would know it would be safe, since she covered every farm in the area with her antibiotic. But she somehow doubted it. She was annoyed with herself for not packing lunch. She definitely knew better and wouldn't be quick to do it again. She thought again about the back of her pink skirt.

It seemed that as soon as she had gotten back to the newspaper, her sandwich was in front of her. She didn't think that the speed in which she got her lunch was necessarily a good thing. She pawed at the sandwich with a grimace.

She never did get back to the newspaper. After she left, as the waitress cleaned the table, she turned the page of the newspaper and sat down humming to herself. Her eyes fell on large print that read "Superbugs Develop from Extreme Antibiotic Overuse."

4

"WOULD YOU LIKE SOME LEMONADE, SWEETIE?" HARVEY asked of his companion.

Pam looked up at him with soft eyes. "I'll take whatever you're making!" They relished in the safety of their new love.

Harvey plucked a sprig of mint from a green plastic window box. He delicately and lovingly placed it on top of the ice cubes in the lemonade glass and sprinkled the top with sugar. He offered it to Pam with gratitude and adoration in his eyes.

As their courtship continued, they regularly attended Reverend Sam's bible class together and always did their homework. The shifts that were occurring in their lives were remarkable. Even Harvey's mom started receiving counseling, and there was talk of them starting to attend one monthly session together. The unorthodox minister continued to draw in increasingly high volumes of people to his classes. There was a shift in energy that was so strong in the church community that people were beginning to talk with excitement.

Every weekend, Harvey and Pam would go to what had become their favorite spot at Juniper Valley Park. There was a set of swings surrounded by trees not far from each of their houses. Harvey would walk over to Pam's house to pick her up and they would walk together to this spot, where they would sit and swing for hours. Sometimes they would sit in silence or chat about their homework. They would read the graffiti from days gone by. On the top bar holding up the swing Harvey read, "Happy Birthday Annavanessa - Nov/Dec 1987." They would make up stories about the people whose words they read. "Annavanessa! Sounds like two little girls who were joined at the hip!" they laughed and laughed.

5

IT WAS 4:00 IN THE MORNING WHEN THE WILD BUNCH finally left Rick's and cruised down Duval Street on the way back to Truman Annex. For reasons they couldn't figure out, and didn't try to, Allie and Noah were left walking alone, side by side down the sparsely lit street. It was still unreasonably humid even at that time of night, or better said, morning. Allie's yellow, flowered sundress clung to her sweaty body like shrink-wrap. In one smooth, fluid motion, Noah swooped down to pick up something from the ground, then shoved it in his pocket, saying, "The directions for my time machine." They both smiled, but said nothing and kept walking. Every time they made eye contact they would both turn away with embarrassment and surprise. After all, the last time they were in each other's regular company, Noah was trying to evict Allie and John from his house. They seemed a very unlikely couple by their own, or anyone else's, account, and this added to the surreal nature of the night. Noah broke the silence. "I've been seeing five-pointed stars everywhere and I've been having this feeling like something is coming."

Allie shrugged her shoulder and gave a gentle wave, "Hi." They looked at each other in silent agreement–there was a very good chance that it was Allie that he felt heading into his life. She squinched her nose and looked up thoughtfully. "Hmm, weird."

"What?" Noah asked with interest.

"Well, it's just that," she stumbled and hesitated, then she finally explained, "I went to a psychic for the first time this weekend and she very specifically and adamantly told me to constantly visualize myself being surrounded by a white light in the form of a five-pointed star." She wondered then if that was so Noah could find her. She continued, "She also told me that there is a graveyard here in town that has five magnetic planes that cross it in such a way that doesn't exist anywhere else. She told me it would be real important for me to go there. My friends aren't really into that kind of stuff, so I didn't go. Do you know where it is?"

Noah thought for a second; he was never very quick to speak. "Yeah, but I think it's pretty far from here."

Allie's thoughts jumped to the paper that Noah put in his pocket a few blocks before. "Can I see the directions for your time machine?" Noah reached into his pocket and handed her what they now realized was a postcard. It was wrinkled and had been bent more than a few times. It had a picture of a muscular man posing in a blue and black leopard Speedo lying on the beach, partway in the water, and read, "Flex on the beach–Florida" in big pink and white letters. Allie turned it over to see the whole back filled with small and strange writing. It was hard to see, but her eye fell on the phrase, "the magnetic zone". Allie froze with confused delight. They had just been talking about the graveyard and its five magnetic planes! They agreed that something was obviously pushing them to the graveyard and strangely enough as they turned the corner, it was right in front of them. Noah said that they might not be able to get in because it was probably locked at night, but they walked on as if they were being led. Exactly in a line in front of them was an opening that had been ripped into the metal fence. Their hearts pounded.

Noah let Allie in first, but then walked in front of her as if he knew where he was going. They came to a place in the walkway where they could make a right or a left. Noah hesitated. Allie took the lead. Not having ever been any-where near there before, she was surprised to feel herself being moved in that direction. Their pace quickened. Allie stopped suddenly and turned right into another sec-tion of the graveyard without knowing why. They walked a few steps and Allie halted, paralyzed and speechless. In the stone walkway was etched a huge five-pointed star! Even in her stunned state, she was moved to walk for-ward. She looked down and etched in the stone was an anchor. She glanced at the postcard again. There was only moonlight to see by, making it difficult to make out any of the finely-printed words. A glitter of light hit the corner of the card. It read, "Ankor bateau". Jesus! What was going on?

Allie's basic foreign language skills led her to believe this could be translated as, "boat or battle anchor". But what she still couldn't begin to figure out was why was this postcard saying, "boat anchor" just as she was standing in front of one?

The string of synchronicities was way more intense than anything she had ever experienced before. Noah was obviously just as dumbfounded. They felt like they were little twigs being pushed by ripples in an ocean of interconnected everythings that were all so much bigger than themselves. They surrendered their thoughts and followed along. Allie held the postcard at arm's distance from her eyes, trying to catch the moonlight. She saw an address. It read, "724 Duval Street". They shrugged their shoulders and helplessly headed to the address. Did they really have a choice?

6

ELI WAS MUTTERING TO HIMSELF THE WHOLE WAY HOME. "Great philosophers ...Hmmf!" This was the first assignment ever that he wasn't bounding home to begin. He was absolutely sure that by focusing on concrete ideas and occurrences, he could figure out an answer.

Kanta started to greet her son with her usual alacrity, then cut herself short when she saw his grumbling face. "Oh, no! What's happened?" she asked with a furrowed brow.

"I just can't understand it! She usually makes so much sense. Now, she's throwing this nebulous philosophical banter at me thinking it offers a real solution!"

Kanta was relieved. When she had first seen his face, she had momentarily forgotten her son's tendency toward melodrama regarding his political projects and thought his demeanor was because of something that was really wrong. She crossed her arms in front of her and moved out of the way, letting him continue mumbling to himself all the way upstairs. She didn't bother to tell him that his father would be late along with dinner. She knew he would lose track of time working on the computer until she called him down.

He grabbed his well-used copy of *Critical Condition–How Health Care in America Became Big Business and Bad Medicine*, by Barlett and Steele. He flipped through the highlighted pages, stopping on page four. "Much of the turmoil is a direct result of a national policy to run health care like a business, a misguided notion promoted by Washington...that the free market and for-profit health care would restrain costs and bring high-quality care to all. On both accounts, the experiment has failed miserably. In the meantime, tens of billions of dollars–money that could have gone into patient care–has been drained from consumers and corporate subscribers, and transferred to investors, executives, and others who have a stake in per-petuating this myth. The result is a chaotic system that has shifted its focus from saving lives to saving dollars; one that discourages preventative medicine and rewards over-testing and over-medicating..."

So there was the problem in a nutshell, but what to do? "Think, think!" he said to himself with a clenched jaw while he thumped his forehead with his hand. He leaned his head backwards and began to roll his neck. He really just wasn't getting anywhere with this. He said aloud, "Please God, help me!" He was surprised by his outburst, not really considering himself religious. The words "think, think," kept echoing through his head. He looked up and his eyes fell on a book that he had never opened before. It had showed up on his doorstep a while ago from an anonymous sender, but after reading the title, he had laughed in disinterest and put it on his shelf with the other hundred books, not having thought about it since.

He now took the book down and with piqued curiosity read the title again slowly: "Think–a Compelling Introduction to Philosophy."

Now, what in the crap was this? He thought again of Mama's suggestion of opening up his scope of research to include the great thinkers. Now, here he was drawn to this book. He thought again of the mysterious way it came to him all that time ago. The coincidences were uncanny. He felt uncomfortable. Whenever he dipped into the place of unexplainable phenomena that challenged his concrete world he felt that same discomfort. Then more of Mama's words echoed through his head: "Get out of the box..." He considered the situation carefully. After a year of research and focus, he hadn't gotten anywhere. He shrugged his shoulders, leaned back in his chair, and opened the book.

7

It was still dark when they got to 724 Duval Street, but it had to be pushing 6:00 a.m. They looked up at the number painted on the glass door and pushed it open. It led to an upstairs outdoor eating area that must have belonged to one of the restaurants. It looked down on Duval Street. Why was the door left open? Allie walked up first and picked up something that she found to be a map of the town. She put the map in her pocketbook without looking at it. At this point, her four-inch platform straw sandals that matched so perfectly with her pocketbook, were in her hand. She hobbled up the stairs with Noah following closely behind. When they got to the top, Noah looked at the postcard with the abundance of streetlight they had available and read, "St. Mary's Star of the Sea". Really now, could they get away from the damn stars? Allie looked at Noah's navy blue shirt. It had a white diagram of constellations. *I guess not,* she thought. She opened the map and right in the middle in big print it read, "St. Mary's Star of the Sea". They looked at each other in exhausted unanimous approval. To St. Mary's they would go!

The sunlight was starting to poke through the night-time sky as they walked to the church. Would it even be open? They had forgotten. It was Memorial Day. The 7:00 a.m. Memorial Service would be beginning shortly. They looked on the postcard and of course it said across the top, "Happy Memorial Wreath May 2000 Day!" It was just ridiculous. They felt like they were in a movie, that all of the details of the night were scripted and they were just playing their parts. They sat in the front pew of the church waiting for who knows what. Allie tried to make out more of the writing. "Ask also for the free Homily of Pepper and the transubstantiation letter from Celeste Smith of Nekenburg–St. Mary's Star of the Sea." Allie showed Noah. It had to be done. She walked up to the altar and requested the Homily of Pepper and transubstantiation letter from the elderly man who was setting up. He looked at her obviously alarmed and walked into the back, disappearing from sight. He never came back out. They agreed that the need for sleep was too strong to continue. They left the church and made their way back to Noah's car. They had decided she would accompany him to drop off the carful of stuff at his apartment. After all, the contents of his car were all the possessions he had left in the world. The day before he'd had a garage sale selling the rest of his stuff, and moved from St. Petersburg, arriving in town the very moment Allie first saw him at Fat Tuesday's. The plan was after dropping his stuff off at his family's compound of apartments, he would then drive them back to the townhouse she had rented with her friends. Boy, did she have a story for them!

As they walked in now broad daylight Allie got a better look at herself. She had bleeding blisters on her feet from her cute shoes, a skinned and bloody knee, and dirty legs from when she fell off a curb into a puddle in a partially drunken episode just hours before she had seen Noah on the street. Her hair and skin were oily from the humidity. The amount of time that had passed since her shower the day before wasn't helping either. She knew her mascara, which she very rarely wore, was smeared all around her eyes. She glanced over herself and looked over at him with apologetic eyes. "I am an absolute mess!"

Noah stared at her with penetrating eyes, "I've never seen anything more beautiful in all my life."

8

ELI WAS DISGUSTED. HE FELT MORE OVERWHELMED THAN ever. This book he felt so drawn to only served to confirm his thoughts about philosophy–that it was tail-chasing crap. Every philosopher would contradict every other philosopher and himself. It also corroborated his point about intuition. He felt led to this book and it was no help. So much for this stupid stuff; he was going to get back to concrete history. He pulled another book off of his shelf called *The Lessons of History*, by Will and Ariel Durant. He flipped through and stopped randomly on a page that had not been folded over or highlighted, and read, "Inequality is an inevitable outcome of freedom. Violent revolutions do not so much redistribute wealth as destroy it. There may be a redivision of the land, but the natural inequality of men soon recreates an inequality of possessions and privileges, and raises to power a new minority with essentially the same instincts as the old. The only real revolution is in the enlightenment of the mind and improvement of character, the only emancipation is individual, and the only real revolutionists are philosophers." He huffed in annoyance, "Now what is this!" He couldn't get away from this philosophy thing! The first part of the passage made sense, but it did give a very grim picture–that history is cyclical and things have not been getting any better; everything just repeats itself. Everything he read seemed to say the same thing. This is just how it is. Nothing can ever change, nor will it. It's impossible. As for the end of the passage, it sounded nice, but it just didn't make any sense, and he was about over the philosopher thing. Just then his mom called for dinner and for once it was a welcome sound.

9

ALLIE'S RETURN HOME WAS BITTERSWEET. SHE LOVED HER home and always loved returning to it , but she was still tingly from her strange experience. *Noah,* she thought, sighing. The last thing she wanted at that point was a relationship, especially a long-distance one. But the magic of that night couldn't be denied. The experience fueled the intuitive opening that had begun months prior. She started reading a book called "Synchronicities" by Carl Jung, which talked about the Cosmic Consciousness and the Collective Unconscious. She started meditating regularly and having out-of-body experiences. She would drive down to Key West almost every weekend to see Noah, and come home and throw herself back into her spiritual studies. She was having an increasingly hard time staying grounded in the material world and more specifically, in her job. All of the ridiculous details of her work seemed more horrifically moronic than ever. She wanted to quit her job and move to Key West. Oddly enough, it was Noah, the person who had inadvertently sparked her full focus on her spiritual path, who was the one who kept her grounded in the "real" world. He would always remind her of what an amazingly good job she had. How most people go their whole lives and could never get a job like it. He reminded her of her five-year plan to get out of her job permanently and urged her to continue on it. "Five years will pass quickly," he reminded her. "You'll be so glad you did it. Then you can screw off and meditate all day if you want." His gentle reasoning resonated with her logical tendencies, and she did her best to stay halfway in both worlds and give each enough focus to keep it all going. They spent hours lying in the tropical Key West paradise defining and redefining the specifics of their individual five-year plans. They spent even more time dreaming about what they would do when they were all done. They both wanted to travel everywhere. They talked about taking a sailboat to the Bahamas, roaming through the Australian outback, and living off the land in the Tahitian Islands. Allie's time with Noah awakened every extreme in her: idealism, focused diligence on financial security, and increasing awareness of the interconnectedness of all things.

In September of 2000, Noah came up to stay with Allie for a few months while he prepared his house, which he had been renting to friends, to be sold. He still had his apartment in Key West, which he shared with his brother, and he had every intention of returning there after the holidays. In October, Allie and Noah went to Key West for Fantasy Fest and when they came home, they brought all of Noah's stuff with them. He made the decision to put a permanent end to their long-distance relationship. Instead of returning back to his Key West life in January 2001, Noah and Allie joined their five-year plans and closed on what would be the first of many pieces of investment real estate.

Part III

1

T{.sc HE} N{.sc EW} Y{.sc EAR'S} ball dropped in T{.sc IMES} S{.sc QUARE} welcoming in 2003. Allie and Noah spent the holidays in their beloved Key West. Their good friends surrounded them and this celebration would become one of their most memorable. As they kissed in a karaoke bar, they were completely unaware of the loud and wild surroundings. A couple passed and put beads around their connected heads. Their business partnership was cruising along like a finely tuned machine. They were halfway into their five-year plan and it was going perfectly according to plan. They now had five properties and were actively looking to procure more. Allie was somehow keeping her energy pretty equally in her two very different worlds. During the day she would sell pharmaceutical drugs to doctors for the people who wanted to take them, and at night she continued to expand her being to understand the ways that she could help the people that wanted more than a band-aid for their deeply-rooted illnesses. She was in a Massage Therapy Program at a school called, "Bhakti School for Intuitive Massage and Healing". She was also enrolling in a Ministerial Program, was partway through an Astrology/Parapsychology Program, and was almost finished with a Naturopathic Doctorate. Her purpose grew clearer by the day, as did her emotions. She knew that at some point she would have a Holistic Healing Practice where she could be in her preferred world of energy and spiritual endeavors most, if not all, of the time.

She knew her days at Centaury were numbered. The situation at the company grew dimmer every month. There were new management practices and a continuously growing movement to remove all of the autonomy and creativity of the reps, supposedly for the purpose of accurate and legal representation of the drugs. There were more initiatives, more spreadsheets that were to provide weekly tracking for the initiatives, and worst of all, there was the IPAQ. Allie called it the "Repstalker" and it was a very accurate description of the new situation. The IPAQ would log in and track the time and details of each sales call. Every night the representatives were to connect it to their telephone line, which would report back to Mother Centaury every specific of the day. And if there were questionable patterns or inconsistencies, there would be hell to pay. Everyone was under close scrutiny. This seemed really ironic to Allie, because if anything should be under close scrutiny, it should be the close affiliations of the members of the upper echelons of pharmaceutical companies with the highest members of government. Maybe someone should be asking why the "non-biased" panel that reviewed drugs for the Food and Drug Administration was made up of thirty-five percent of people from Big Pharma. It used to be that Centaury would hire intelligent, motivated, passionate people and then trust their judgment as to the best ways to organize the territories.

All the reps would joke that they should just hire monkeys, because they were being paid so much to do what now could best be described as completely mindless work.

Allie had increasing discomfort with the amount that reps were paid. What were they actually doing for all of that money? Was it helping to increase the health care standards in the country? Were people really getting better, or were they just becoming more dependent on more drugs? These questions, and the general chaos of the pharmaceutical world, were really wearing down Allie's capacity to keep everything going. She listened to stories of doctors having affairs with reps, and the reps market share numbers going up accordingly. She watched as ten drug commercials an hour would captivate billions of viewers. Fishing trips for doctors by reps, although technically illegal, were common. She even heard one story about diversion of pharmaceutical company funds for the company of prostitutes on one such fishing charter. That was probably the most shocking one of all, and she was grateful that at least the story didn't implicate *her* company. She took a vacation to Costa Rica and in the airport she saw a huge lighted sign for Centaury Pharmaceuticals. Next to it was a sign for Senecox, explaining its magnificence in Spanish. The domination of the United States Pharmaceutical Industry spread across borders and languages.

2

THE HARMONIOUS SPINNING OF GRACE AVILA'S PERFECT world came to a screeching halt in less than one minute. It took her some time to process what had just happened. Her manager asked her to destroy legal documents, illegally refrain from reporting information, and lie. He did more than ask her, he told her. Is this happening? She was dumbfounded. She was struck blind by the audacity, and in the same instant was filled with fear. Who would believe her over this older person who was so well established in the company. Did he really think this could be covered up?

Grace mentally reviewed the situation. A farmer had given her information on what seemed to be a new strain of infection that had broken out in his flock of chickens. He told her about it because he believed it to be an adverse event from her drug, Pylobact. He was thinking that it may be a new strain of infection that was resistant to even the most effective antibiotic, which in this market was her drug. He was actually concerned that it could be the very early start of an epidemic. The relationship he had with Grace was strong. He trusted her and knew that she epitomized the ideal role of a drug rep—a liaison of accurate, pertinent information between the company and the market. He knew that Grace and Millennium Pharmaceuticals had a legal obligation to report all adverse event information to the FDA. In this case, there would be more authorities that would probably be interested, but he wasn't well versed on government. He knew that Grace would follow through and call on him when she had figured out the proper authorities to put him in further contact with.

Grace had a field visit with her manager the day after the report, so she went over the details with him to get a game plan together. She would then go and call the Millennium Customer Service Center Event Reporting Line, and whatever additional agencies that were relevant to this potentially time-sensitive information. That's when it happened. She still couldn't believe it. Her manager, Tim Wagner, explained that he would take care of it and she was to skip the usual protocol. She was to tell the farmer that it was taken care of and that she would be in touch soon. This alarming event brought her to even more horrifying thoughts. What were they trying to cover up? Did he really think that he had the power to keep this information secret? Were people's lives in danger? What had she done?

3

ANOTHER YEAR OF FRUITLESS RESEARCH PASSED QUICKLY FOR Eli. He would soon be turning seventeen. In one more year, he would be graduating from high school. He had been so wrapped up in the whatever-it-was that he had been so absorbed in, that he wasn't even thinking about, or preparing for, college. He decided it was time to lay it all out on the table and get Mama to help him. She had always been so good at leading him along, planting seeds and letting him cultivate them, empowering him to educate himself. But, he had hit a roadblock and needed more than some gentle prodding. Instead of packing his book bag with his school books that morning, he filled it with many of his research notebooks and most studied books from over the years of this project. As he plodded up to her bench, feeling beaten, she sensed his defeat. Of course, she didn't view it the same way as he did. She withheld her usual greeting and follow-up taunting, and looked at him with gentle eyes. He had never seen this side of her, but he appreciated it so much at that moment. He took out each book and flipped through, summarizing his notes and thoughts on each. Then he explained his concerns about college: that he doesn't even want to study Political Science anymore, he hasn't told his parents, he's been avoiding picking colleges, and he feels directionless.

She said, "You can't be in faith and fear at the same time, and you get to choose which you want. Which one sounds more appealing to you?" He nodded his head in concession that obviously faith would be far preferable. "Good!" she said with a slight twinge of possible provocation coming back into her speech. "You have some homework. I'll warn you in advance that you won't see the relevance now, but I can promise that you will when you've finished. Deal?" He nodded again in concession. "Okay. Start studying all of the world religions you can, and find their common strands." She had been hoping that he would have progressed to this on his own from philosophy studies, but sometimes people needed a little more than small pushes along their paths, even a little more than subtle Divine Intervention, which often goes unrecognized. Sometimes they need a divine butt-whooping.

"Now one more thing before you go," Mama called out to him. He stopped in his tracks with expectant ears. "Remember that it is easier for God to help you if you surrender your free will by asking for his help." Eli shook his head in acknowledgement and left.

Feeling satisfied that he had a solid direction towards *something*, he skipped off. But he didn't go straight home. He stopped at the library and started his new mission. He loved to have a mission. This was actually a mission within a mission, which was even better! Before he stepped inside, he remembered what Mama said and looked up to the sky thoughtfully. "Please help me to see clearly my path and purpose, and be brave enough to follow it." He quickly found the Religious Studies section and started a pile on the floor of his selections. His eyes moved swiftly over the titles. In five minutes, he had five books: *The Tibetan Book of the Dead*, encompassing Buddhists beliefs; *Tao Te Ching*, which covered Chinese mysticism; *The Essential Kabbalah*, which explained the primary aspects of Jewish Mysticism; *The Bhagavad-Gita*, an essential Hindu text; and *The Bible*, including Old and New Testaments. Like Mama said, he didn't understand where it was going, but at least it was something more concrete than mere philosophical banter. He had a strange feeling that he couldn't immediately describe. He stood staring off into space for a while trying to put it into words. It was a feeling of expansiveness. He felt himself take a deep breath and let out a big sigh. Something had shifted in him, something that he wasn't in a place to understand yet. A feeling of peace washed over him, and he carefully picked up his pile and made his way to check out. There wasn't any room left in his book bag, so he carried his new gems by hugging them close to his chest to support the weight. He came into the house with a smile. Kanta was surprised and curious, but didn't ask. She felt the peace emanating off of him and talking didn't seem to matter.

4

"Pamela, do you accept this man to be your lawful wedded husband, to have and to hold, through richer and poorer, until death do you part?"

Pam gazed into Harvey's eyes with adoration. "I do".

"I now pronounce you man and wife. You may kiss the bride."

Harvey and Pam sank to the deepest, most spectacular kiss they had ever experienced. When they came to, they didn't know how long they had been in that special place but realized it was time to walk back down the aisle of the church.

As they approached the waiting white wedding limo, rice flew and birds chirped. The sky was cloudless and the most perfect shade of blue anyone had ever remembered seeing.

It was the happiest day of their lives.

Part IV

1

IN AN INSTANT, IT WAS OVER: THE JOB, THE SECURITY, AND the foundation for all of her previous plans. But she felt no sorrow. She didn't really feel anything. It couldn't be described as numbness. It was more like neutrality. Neutrality was the magic word. She watched the feelings as they came. She felt them pass through her. She let them wash over her like a wave and then she watched them flow away. She didn't get sucked in, brought down, absorbed, or ruled. It was utterly amazing. Her senses were supercharged. She could smell better, taste deeper, and see with her eyes closed. The crispness of the air trickled over her like it was in slow motion. It didn't make sense not to use logic. It didn't jive with the long-held process of analysis and deep scrutinization that everything would usually have to pass through to get her approval for her actions. But it didn't matter. She was free.

It was January 7, 2004, and Allie had just given her two-week notice at Centaury. It was all so odd. She thought about the details of this major life change. She had just retired from the corporate life and world. After five years of "service", she was now considered a Centaury "retiree", pension and everything. So what if the pension money didn't come for another thirty plus years. She was even ahead of her own five-year plan for herself, which she started to implement after a year or so of being under the grip of Centaury's massive talons. She had originally wanted to wait to leave Centaury until she had opened her Holistic Healing Practice and had an established base of clientele. This, she had figured, would coincide with the end of the original five-year plan. But apparently, God had a different plan for her. Once she switched her focus to aligning her will with the Divine Will, things really started to cook. It was like everything was sped up. She was sure now that she could have left Centaury even earlier if she would have been able to get out of her left brain quicker and not been hell-bent on her adherence to *her* plan. But, it took her some time of being on her spiritual path to sort it out. If she'd learned anything on her spiritual quest, it was that God's plan for us is always easier, lighter and infinitely better than our plans for ourselves. It was the process of staying in a place of faith-based focus in the divine plan, instead of her own fear-driven ego-based plan, that she was intently focused on now. She realized that if she ever felt feverishly inclined to go out and create something for herself, it was only because she was not in a place of trusting what was in store for her and being open the Highest Plan. She became aware that everything she had created for herself had been created out of fear: fear that she would be dependent on her parents, or worse yet, a man; fear that she would always have to do work she didn't like; fear that she would have to live under circumstances that kept her spirit bound up; or fear of a thousand other equally as frightening things. She decided to make a conscious effort that from now on, she would try to create everything from faith–faith in her highest expression of self-faith in the Highest Plan.

She was still working on the feeling of dichotomy, which she now best explained by right brain and left brain pull. When she was at Centaury, her left brain pushed her into her real estate ventures to create the financial stability she would need to leave her job and start her new business. Her right brain knew that real estate was just the physical manifestation of her God-given abundance. If it weren't through real estate, the money and security would come some other way. Then, when she swung too much in that direction, her logic would tell her, "If you buy this many houses that are appreciating at this percentage, you will create such and such an amount of assets," and on and on it went. But it didn't matter. No matter how it happened, she retired at twenty-nine.

Her definition of being retired was different than a full-time left-brainer, and different than what she used to believe. She knew that she wouldn't ever have to work at a job she didn't like, and that all the work she did would be intuitively-based instead of logic-based. She knew that she would love her work so much that she would never again feel like she was working. She had enough money to last her many years without working at all if she wanted to continue selling off her assets. Any work she did would be out of love for it, which never mind the actual money, is what she felt it really meant to be retired.

Allie had a brand new life. She went from working full time, plus buying and managing real estate acquisitions, four different school programs, and trying to take the best care of herself possible, to just taking care of herself and the houses. It was like a permanent vacation. What would she do with all that time? Before she did anything, she decided to take herself to Hawaii for two weeks as a congratulatory present for fearlessly leaving her job and focusing completely on her spiritual path. Days were now spent in a leisurely fashion and it was the weirdest thing! In June 2004, her Massage License came through. She was legally able to have a Healing Practice using Energy Work under this Massage License in the State of Florida. She found the most perfect place to rent space. It was just five minutes from her house, and had wonderful people and great energy. Everything was just as she pictured, and she loved every second of it.

She sat in her yard watching the birds land on the dock and the boats pass. It really was beautiful. She noticed it so much more now that she had time to enjoy it. She used to sit longingly at her desk getting glimpses of the scene outside through the slats in the wide wood blinds which stretched between her and the aquatic wonderland. Now, she sat outside feeling fulfilled. *All the work was so worth it!* she thought, smiling, remembering Noah's words years before. She observed the thickness of the foliage, all of which she and Noah had planted during their years there. It wasn't always so beautiful. When they got into the lease option for the house and moved in, it was a real dump, whose only saving graces were its placement on the water, its proximity to the beach, and a huge fireplace that was the focal gathering point for the house. Since those three things were pretty good saving graces, they went into the lease happily and dealt with the other not-so-desirable things as best they could.

After a while of doing real estate, they knew that they had to get property that would appreciate the most, which in their area would be beach property and more specifically, waterfront. Waterfront did not necessarily have to mean beachfront, it could mean on a canal. Noah was the bigger search engine in their acquisitions operation, and found this goldmine of an opportunity in an ad in the newspaper. It read: "Lease to own $239,900; $1,650 per month..." He told Allie about it and they drove the couple of minutes it took from where they lived. Upon entering, they knew immediately it would be their home. Fortunately, they could see past the horrendous and mismatched flooring, awful kitchen, and unforgivable bathroom. When they walked outside for the first time, their bellies stirred with excitement. As usual, Noah was ready to move forward and Allie put her excitement aside for a little while to work out the numbers on the calculator that she always had nearby. The mortgage at her house where they lived was only $560. It was a noteworthy jump to the new lease amount. They went home and continued the careful consideration process. They remembered that the amount of money spent per month would be like forced savings, and the house would appreciate so much more than the amount they would shell out that it would be worth it.

They had been 'stalking' (as they liked to call their process of looking for houses) Madeira Beach for a while. They knew that Redington Shores, just north of it, and Treasure Island, just south of it, were all untouchable for investment and continuing to appreciate rapidly. Even though Madeira Beach had the highest concentration of "crack" arrests in the county, they knew it was only going to be a matter of time before it had to move up to equal the neighboring beaches in property values. They did the math on that and looked at each other knowingly. This decision would be a major part of the "plan". They went back to look at the house again (it had been left open for this purpose) and walked into the backyard. It was now nighttime and the first thing they saw was a huge lighted cross from the Church by the Sea across the canal. This was the final confirmation they needed, and at that moment the decision was made.

All of these memories washed over her and it seemed like she had been sitting in her favorite Nags Head hammock rocking chair for years. She and Noah would joke about their rocking chairs and the amount of time they spent in them. "A little young for that," they would say. She realized she should check the time. She had a session at the office in the afternoon. Six months had elapsed between the time she left Centaury and the time she was officially seeing clients at the office, and getting back on a time schedule took some remembering.

She was always surprised and delighted to see how each session would progress. She seemed to be evolving weekly, as did the nature of her work. If someone would have ever told her logical brain, even a year ago, that she would be putting her hands on a person's arm and they would feel better she would accuse them of smoking crack, and would have never believed them. She believed it could be done back then, but not that she would be doing it. Now, barely anything that happened in session, or as a result of sessions, sounded strange to her. She had come such a long way, but it had also been a really long process. She called herself an Integrative Healing Facilitator, because she didn't want to take any credit for a person's healing process. She believed she was a channel for healing energy from the Universe that the person's higher self used to heal themselves with. She created the space for healing and the person would connect with their

Higher Source, whatever they wanted to call it: God, God-dess, The Universe, The All-That-Is, or whatever else people felt comfortable with. She had been raised Catholic, so the words "Jesus" and "God" were comfortable for her, but she believed that Jesus taught non-judgment, and that it wasn't her place to judge people's understandings of the Higher Order of things. It was her job to help people evolve back into the remembrance of the oneness of God's arms that Free Will made them think they left.

She chuckled as she thought of the fact that she was actually a minister. Reverend Allie Kramer, ordained in the Order of Melchizedek the same way as most ministers in Christian-based belief systems were. She laughed, not because of her lack of sincerity in her work, but on the contrary, her ministry was definitely her life. However, she just wasn't your typical minister. She was tall and thin with long blonde hair and a penchant for hip-hop music, and until recently would drink and cuss like a sailor. That was one of the many amazing things she attributed to her work. She had wanted to stop drinking for so many years, but was unsuccessful. Then one day, it just went away. She didn't change her friends or surroundings, but the need for fulfillment from sources other than her Higher Source was magically disappearing with little or no direct effort. It had been the same thing with her diet. She had always eaten the worst kind of crap all the time and because of her beast-like metabolism, she never gained any weight. So, there was no deterrent to dissuade her from the terrible practice. But then one day, it just changed. She always liked to refer to the healing process as "insidious". It just sort of crept up on you.

Her mind went back to the session today. She absolutely loved her work. She knew how lucky she was to be one of the few that really felt that way. She would always start her workout with a person by telling them to come in with a "wish list" of everything they would love to see in their lives, no holds barred. Many of the common constituents of a list were: have more peace, handle stress more gracefully and in a more healthy way, feel better, lose weight, get off of medications, heal old relationship patterns and make new healthy ones, heal internal patterns of addiction in any form–alcohol, drugs, over or under-eating, shopping, etc. She saw that 100% of the people that came in for their sessions regularly and did their homework, all had their lives completely change for the better, and were able to cross the old things off their list and make new lists. Whatever was happening in session was definitely dealing with not only the physical, but also the emotional, mental, and spiritual aspects of healing, and it really, really worked.

The nature of the work was really strange and the way she explained what it was she was actually doing came out different every time. One way that seemed to come up a lot to describe the work was the perspective of the body as an electric circuit. The body is an electric circuit. That's why whenever you hold the end of a live wire, you get electrocuted. That's why when the heart stops, a defibrillator can sometimes spark it back up. That's why with Kiriligian photography the aura can be seen. Seeing energy in and around the body wasn't her specialty, but she could definitely feel and translate it, and then act as a conductor to get light into the areas where it needed to be. She likened it to an old house with wiring that was severed or frayed in different places, which caused certain circuits to not connect and made certain fixtures not work. It was the same way with the body. The body has the capacity to heal itself. Take a wound for example. The body knows the sequence and details of what to do to heal it. The body has that capacity for all wounds, even if they are mental or emotional. Time, stress, pollutants and toxins, and a build-up of unexpressed emotion, all fray the circuits in the body and interferes with the innate healing system. All of this is based in quantum physics, she would explain. Everything comes down to vibration. Every part of our body has a certain vibration that could be measured if it were hooked up to an oscilloscope (a device that measures vibration). For instance, a healthy appendix measures eighty-two hertz. Emotions, such a fear and anger, also have a vibration, which interfere with the normal vibration of the body. The healing process would often be likened to the peeling back of layers of an onion. The most superficial energies would have to be healed to get into the core source of the problems.

She also started using astrology to help with understanding the core issues to be dealt with. The idea of astrology was never of interest to Allie in the past, but studying, understanding, and utilizing it now was a natural progression. When she first had an interest in it, she took a correspondence class. It seemed like it was too vague and full of scathing generalizations to be of any practical use to anyone, much like any normal newspaper horoscope. It wasn't until she had become adept at working with the energetic aspects of things that she was able to really get it. Now, she could look at a chart and mesh her intuition with her book knowledge to help people move along their spiritual paths. There was something to be said for the idea of reading all the books and then throwing them out as if they didn't exist. As amazingly right-on as astrology was in her work, she understood that she couldn't make any of the things she studied in this lifetime the be-all end-all of systems. She knew she had to be able to look at everything and know there was still so much more than she could ever understand, and be open to The Indescribable, The Undeniable, The Divine. "We are so limited by our vocabulary," she and her friends would always say. The things that really mattered, the levels on which they were working to really heal, were things that they could never explain with words.

2

ALL OF A SUDDEN, ELI WAS CONNECTED TO THE WELLSPRING of universal consciousness, just for a second, then it was gone. But once he had a taste of it, he knew it would become his lifelong mission to attain it permanently. It was the strangest thing he could ever imagine. In an instant, he was automatically tuned in to the archives of infinite forever. He understood things that he was never familiar with before. He saw energy flowing from the past to the present, then the future, in one circuit, as if they were really all the same thing. He understood the incomprehensible. He knew what he had to do.

Kanta and Tanti sat with bated breath trying to imagine what Eli could be so serious about. He asked them to come into the living room and sit down, at which point he just stared at them. He didn't even have the nervous fidget that was customary for him. The silence was more than uncomfortable, and his parents looked at each other for silent emotional support. After what seemed like eons, Eli finally spoke. "I'm not going to college." It was even a little surprising to hear himself say it. He had been leaning towards switching his major, but it had never in a million years occurred to him that he would not ever go to college.

It was interesting to see the very opposite reactions that his parents had to the same statement. Kanta gave a big sigh, putting her hand up to her sternum like the weight of the world was removed from her. Tanti tensed up, his face and neck turning crimson, and clenched his fists together. "What do you mean? What are you saying?" he forced out through pursed lips and closed jaw.

Eli wasn't even frazzled. He wasn't even stressed. "I'm on to something. I'm on to something real big. An answer. An answer to all the problems that I've been hoping to have solved."

Tanti was getting more wild-eyed by the second. "What does that have to do with your education, your foundation for a future full of options? Do you think I would ever have gotten a job doing work I love to do while being able to support my family if I wouldn't have gotten an education?"

For once, Eli wasn't tempted to get into, and win, a verbal war with his dad. "I didn't expect you to understand."

While all this was going on, Kanta sat back in to the comfort of the couch with her hands folded in her lap, trying not to smile. "Go to your room!" Tanti blurted, flailing his arms and hands in helpless aggravation.

Eli went to his room still feeling so different, so light. If it were God's grace at work, boy, was it a powerful force. He picked a book from his new pile and started reading. Hours passed and he was still reading. He had pages of notes and had started a comparison chart. The first thing he noticed was that every major religion had a single form of God at the head of the belief system, even where there are many Gods, or forms of the same God present. They all have some form of prayer, teachings, rituals, and rules of behavior. All have sacred sites that are revered by followers of that religion. Some are specific geographical locations and some are shrines built anywhere. All have guidelines and explanations for life, death and after-death.

His eyes started closing. Every night it was the same thing, for as far back as he could remember. He would read until his eyes literally closed. He moved his pile of books off the bed and onto the floor next to it. Before he drifted off to sleep, he remembered something he had read about giving the subconscious mind a specific problem to work on while you are asleep. He couldn't remember how exactly it worked, but it was something about harnessing the powerful moments before you go to sleep by setting an intention for problem solving. Apparently, the mind would follow along in the direction that you led it during that time and upon awakening, you would have your answer. He read that this capacity would get stronger with nightly repetition, and with the writing down of the dreams and awareness so that the language of dreams could better be understood. He set the intention to come to more realizations along his spiritual path quicker and with less effort on his part, to understand the nature of things without having to do years of research to get to one big "ah-ha". Specifically for this night, he wanted to streamline his comparative religion project by understanding what he was supposed to without reading anything else or making any more charts. He drifted off to sleep with a knowing smile.

Upon arising, he went to start his normal routine when he remembered the new pattern he wanted to start.

He grabbed his notebook that he had now designated as his dream journal, and looked up trying to remember something, anything, that happened while he was asleep.

3

GRACE DROVE FAST WITH HER MIND REELING FASTER THAN
it ever had. Little clips of her experience at Millennium
flashed before her. She remembered back to her first melt-
down when she worried if she was really hurting more
people than she was helping. She couldn't remember
what exactly it was that made her feel better, but she suddenly picked up on a Millennium pattern–whenever anyone would have a concern, there would be a perfect
presentation of words that were flawlessly strung together
with a confident demeanor by someone in the company
who was revered, a doctor of this or that, and all worries
would go away. How did they do that? Well, she knew
something was really up this time and no words, no subtle threats, no nothing would keep her from the truth.

After what seemed like eternities of driving, Grace got
home. This night she skipped her usual lengthy nighttime
work routine and got right online. She was glad that she
hadn't reacted emotionally when her manager was there.
She wasn't known for emotional control, but she'd pulled
it off this time and would have to for a while longer until
she could get together a plan. She decided that she could

better research the situation from inside the company than by leaving immediately like she really wanted to. She hesitated as she went to start her research. She was familiar with the idea of antibiotic resistance and Superbugs, but had always thought the good of antibiotics drastically outweighed the potential negatives. She was now determined to open up to a clearer picture of the situation. The first website she came to was: http://www.sierra-club.org/factoryfarms/antibiotics/health.asp. She pulled her computer into her lap and leaned back on her new, taupe, micro-fiber couch, and read:

"How Livestock Antibiotics Threaten Our Health: using antibiotics to promote livestock growth could cause substantial ecological problems that could threaten public health." - Erica Frank, M.D., M.P.H. Associate Professor Emory University School of Medicine; national board member, Physicians for Social Responsibility.

Small, family-owned livestock farms have been replaced by giant factory farms that crowd thousands of hogs, chickens and cows into industrial barns, generate vast amounts of animal manure, and use antibiotics to promote faster animal growth. Unlike traditional family farming methods, this industrial style of meat production causes severe water and air pollution, and threatens public health by reducing the ability of antibiotics to cure infectious diseases in humans. A Dangerous Cycle!

Drugs Are Routinely Added to Livestock Feed

About one-third of the antibiotics used in the United States each year, roughly 16 million pounds, is routinely added to animal feed to speed the growth of livestock. Antibiotics have been used in the production of many of the meat and poultry products available in conventional grocery stores. This practice poses unnecessary risks to the health of our families.

Consumers May Be Exposed to Deadly Bacteria

Routinely exposing bacteria to antibiotics allows naturally drug-resistant bacteria to survive, reproduce and spread. Consumers may be exposed to drug-resistant Salmonella, E. coli, Campylobacter and other potentially deadly bacteria through the consumption of contaminated food or untreated water.

Essential Antibiotics May Become Ineffective

Medical professionals rely on many of the same antibiotics used on livestock to treat infectious diseases in humans. If the disease-causing bacteria have become resistant, the drugs don't work. Antibiotic-resistant bacteria make infectious diseases more difficult to treat, leaving humans vulnerable to life-threatening illnesses and increasing the cost of treatment.

The potential danger is growing fast. For example, in a 1997 study from the Centers for Disease Control and Prevention, more than one-third of the reported cases of a particular type of Salmonella that causes food poisoning were caused by Salmonella bacteria resistant to five important antibiotics used to treat the disease. The percentage of resistant bacteria was negligible when this type of Salmonella was studied in 1980. Drug resistance in Campylobacter bacteria, the most commonly known cause of bacterial food-borne illness in the United States, increased from zero in 1991, to 20 percent in 1999.

Health Organizations Raise Concerns

In 1997, the World Health Organization called for a ban on using antibiotics to promote livestock growth. Other public health agencies, including the U.S. Centers for Disease Control and Prevention, have raised concerns about administering medically vital antibiotics to fatten livestock. The European Union heeded these concerns in 1998 when it banned adding human-use antibiotics to animal feed, but the United States has failed to act.

Antibiotics are among the most important public health innovations of the 20th century. They have saved countless lives. It is vital to preserve the effectiveness of these drugs to treat human diseases. Using antibiotics to make livestock grow faster makes it more likely that bacteria will become resistant, and that the antibiotics we need to protect health will become ineffective. The Food and Drug Administration should take immediate action to stop this unnecessary use of antibiotics.

What you can do to stop the unnecessary use of antibiotics on factory farms:

If you eat meat, purchase antibiotic-free products, or organic meat. If your grocer does not offer meats produced without antibiotics, ask for them.

Write a letter to U.S. Food and Drug Administrator, Dr. Jane Henney. This agency is considering restrictions on antibiotics used to promote livestock growth, but faces opposition from drug manufacturers and the livestock industry, which fears lower profits because it would lengthen the time needed to raise animals. Ask Dr. Henney to follow the European Union and leading public health agencies, and ban the use of antibiotics to fatten livestock when those drugs are also used to treat humans. Write to her at the Food and Drug Administration, 5630 Fishers Lane, Room 1061, Rockville, MD 20852.

Contact Your Member of Congress: How to Contact Your Member of Congress About Antibiotic Use in Livestock.

For more information about the Sierra Club's opposition to factory livestock production, **contact us.**

Resources on antibiotic-resistant bacteria:

"Protecting the Crown Jewels of Medicine: A Strategic Plan to Preserve the Effectiveness of Antibiotics," a report by the Center for Science in the Public Interest. Available at http://www.cspinet.org/reports/abiotic.htm, or by calling (202) 332-9110.

"Wow," she said out loud. She had become queasy and put her computer back on the coffee table not knowing if she was going to have to dash for the bathroom. She saw the flaw in the logic. All this time she had been looking at it the wrong way. The premise on which she went to work for Millennium, and her subsequent sales presentations, were based on the fact that there were bacteria in poultry that cause serious human harm, so by using the antibiotics, *her* antibiotics, the food supply, and hence the human population, would be safer. God, it was so simple it made her brain hurt, so how had she missed it? She understood now that the drugs only killed the more benign bacteria populations, leaving the stronger ones to proliferate. She *was* public enemy #1!

"Okay," she reasoned to herself, "if this is so obvious, then how are meat companies/farmers getting away with it? And why is the government going along with it?" It seemed clear that better farming conditions would take care of much of the problem, so why wasn't organic farming mandatory? She started to think about the implications of all of this. Just then the phone rang and it was Allie.

"Hi!" Grace chirped.

"Hi, back at you," Allie peeped.

"Your timing is impeccable, as usual," Grace reported, and then took about an hour to fill her in on the events and follow-up research leading up to the time of the call. Allie listened to everything carefully and added, "Remember about four years ago I got Salmonella and was in the hospital for four days?" How could Grace forget? Upon hearing the news, she immediately drove all the way to the hospital to stay with her. "Well, my digestion hasn't been right since and through studying all of this naturopathic stuff I have come to understand the process and the deterioration of my digestion system, and have been carefully trying to fix the mess. I also understand now that I was likely predisposed to falling prey to the Salmonella because of all of the antibiotics I was put on as a kid and teenager. My immune system was still compromised." Allie was one of many millions, maybe billions, of people that had their own health struggle on account of the conditions. She was one of the lucky ones for two reasons: she didn't die from it, and she was actually aware now of the damage it caused and was actively trying to reverse the process. Most people that were affected probably didn't even know that certain bacteria were a factor in their enigmatic health problems.

It had been a while since Grace and Allie had talked and strangely enough in the gap of time between their contact, Allie and Noah had become convinced of the importance of eating organic foods and had switched over at least half of their grocery purchases to organic. As they chatted, they kept reiterating their disbelief at the fact that the government would allow food standards to be so low as to be dangerous.

"We might really be on to something here," Allie suggested slyly.

"What are you getting at?" Grace urged.

"Well, it seems that the public has a legitimate case against the tobacco companies for their secret reckless endangerment of tobacco users, and although it hasn't really been focused on yet, consumers probably could consider holding the FDA accountable for their lack of diligence with their protection of consumers on the issues of drugs and food, as well. All this being said, there seems to be a similar situation here. How could the makers of antibiotics *not* know that this is happening? It has been well documented for eons. So how, then, could the FDA be oblivious to this?"

"That was a mouthful!" Grace teased, still stunned at the magnitude of all of it.

"Seriously!" Allie continued with increasing fervor. "This is really something. The job of the FDA is to be more knowledgeable about the topics it covers so that it can protect us. That is obviously not happening here and it really has caused the beginning of a nationwide health epidemic. It is so much bigger than just the antibiotic issue. The soil is being stripped bare by unconscientious farming, and there isn't anyone watch-dogging this process. Where do the nutrient contents in food come from? The nutrients aren't just *born* there, the plant pulls in the vitamins and minerals from the soil, but if no regard is given to alternating crop types to replenish the soil with the nutrients, then the food will be void of health value, which is the current trend. There has been an astronomical decrease in the nutrient value of crops over the last 30 years. Ooh, I'm on a real tirade now!"

"You go, girl!" Grace chuckled, still taking it all in.

They said their goodbyes, promising to not let so much time pass *this* time.

Grace thought about Allie's analogy between Big Tobacco and Big Pharma and, the body that tied them together, the FDA. She felt like she was on to something big. She resolved herself to stay at her job and act normal, but document with as much detail as possible the sequence of events so that when the time came to do something, she would be ready.

Part V

1

September 30, 2004

NEWSFLASH...WORLDWIDE RECALL OF SENECOX BY CENTAURY PHARMACEUTICALS BECAUSE OF CONFIRMED LINK TO CARDIO-VASCULAR EVENTS AND DEATH

2

ALLIE HAD JUST WALKED IN FROM YOGA WHEN THE PHONE rang. She smiled as she thought of her new leisurely life without Centaury where she could be just coming in from yoga at that time of day.

"Hello," she sang.

"Allie, are you sitting? Please sit...are you sitting yet?" Grace fumbled out nervously.

"Yeah, okay. Yes, I am. What? Is everything all right?"

"I know you don't watch TV and...well...I thought someone had better...I had better tell you-Senecox was just pulled off of the market today because of a study that proves its link to cardiovascular events and death. I'm sorry. Oh, gosh , did you know? Are you okay?"

Allie went pale with terror. Almost five years of defending her drug from what she thought to be lying competitors talking about Senecox killing people, and it really was! She couldn't believe it. She couldn't speak.

"Allie, please say something. Listen, you didn't know. There is no way you could have known. This isn't your fault. It really isn't your fault."

Allie finally broke her silence with a gasp and streaming tears. "No, it can't be. It isn't right. It must be a mistake. I...I...can't"

"You didn't know. You didn't know!"

"I've caused people to die, families to be destroyed, and dreams to end. I'll never get over this. Oh God, please!"

As the initial shock and denial started to wear off, Allie became angry.

"They must have known! How could they not have known? How can they get away with this? They tricked us. I don't know how far up the sales chain it went, but a lot of people should feel really violated."

"Well, as usual, we are living parallel lives, because this is the same exact situation I'm dealing with in my world. It's these big companies in cahoots with government figures and/or governmental institutions, and it has to stop." Then she gasped with frustrated desperation, "Allie, can we make it stop?"

The determination in her voice was growing. "If it were any other two people, the answer might be different, but these two people have everything it takes to be catalysts for there to really be a chance. We are guided by purity, and idealism, and connection to our Higher Source, and that, my friend, is a force to be reckoned with!"

After relaying the news to Noah, Allie sat alone, her usually notable good posture crumpled over in a heap. She said out loud, shaking her head, "This is a really tough pill to swallow." She remained there, absorbed in the bitter irony, staring through the wood slats at the really green grass.

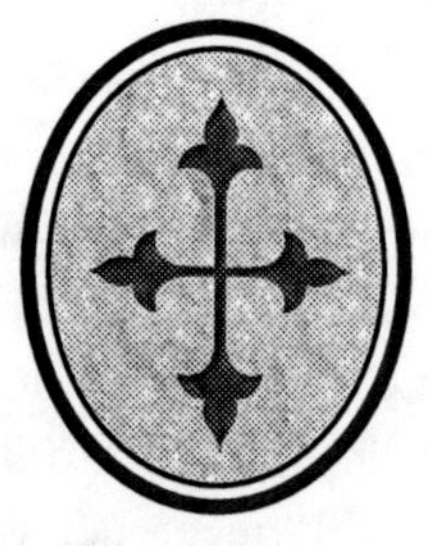

3

NEWSFLASH...PENNSYLVANIA CHEMIST INSTITUTIONALIZED...IT WAS HE WHO ORIGI-NALLY CREATED SENECOX COMPOUND...

4

KANTA STOOD OVER HER SON'S BED TRYING TO KEEP HER emotions contained. "Eli, wake up. Please wake up, hunny."

"Mom! What? Is something wrong? What time is it?" Eli whispered.

"Sit up, son."

Her voice and demeanor made him know it couldn't be good.

"Are you okay? Where's Dad?"

"That's the thing...dear...oh, I'm so sorry. Dad is going to be away for a little while. He's not well. I heard some noise shortly after going to bed and I got up to find him with a bottle of sleeping pills, and he was about to take them. All of them. He needs some help that we can't give him right now."

"No! But why? No...Mom? I don't understand."

"Well, I'm sure you heard about the Senecox recall by Centaury Pharmaceuticals. Well...that was one of his, what did you call them...babies?"

"Oh, my God," Eli groaned. He hunched over in the fetal position and started rocking.

5

About six weeks had passed since the news, and Allie was still having a hard time dealing with the situation. She tried to console herself through her spiritual exercises and tried to keep focused on the bigger picture, but she couldn't help but think about the people that were affected at the individual level. People who were once able-bodied that may now be incapacitated, their families having to shift everything in their lives to take care of them, and worse yet, the survivors of the ones who died. She remembered back to a book about her experience in the pharmaceutical industry that she had written just a few pages of years ago, and knew this could be one way for her to make a contribution in return for all the damage she caused by selling Senecox for so long. Her mind kept flitting back to the book over the last month and a half, but she hadn't felt ready to deal with it just yet. As she thought about this, her cell phone rang and she recognized the number as that of Noah's sister, Nani. She cheerfully answered, not wanting to pull her down, too.

"Hey...what's up?"

"Allie, Hi!"

They briefly caught up on general things and then said, "It's a strange coincidence, really, but my friend has a cousin whose wife recently died, and they are linking her death to Senecox. I told them about you and the book you started writing a while ago, and he wants to talk to you. I hope you don't mind; I gave him your number."

They always seemed to be connected even if they hadn't had contact in a long time, and this conversation was no exception. Allie felt that familiar brewing of something so much bigger than herself. Nani didn't even know Allie was thinking about writing the book again; she remembered it from the years ago when Allie started it.

"Sure, yes, of course, no problem ," Allie stuttered. "I don't know what I could possibly say to him, but have him call for sure."

"Okay, just so you know who it is when he calls, his name is Harvey Akers."

6

AFTER LAYING IN BED FOR DAYS, ELI WAS FINALLY ABLE TO come down to the kitchen. He sat at the table across from his mother and said, "I want to see Dad. I have to tell him some things. I have to tell him it's all right. All of this stuff that I've been working on has helped to give me a different perspective on things in life, and I want to share it with him. We can work together to make a difference, to change the system. I used to look down on him for being so blind to the ridiculousness of the machine he was a part of, but I see it so differently now. I understand that everyone is a summation of their life experience, and each person becomes a slave to their unconscious drives from that experience...that is, until they become aware of it. Awareness changes everything. Awareness is the ticket out. I have a ticket with his name on it, Mom. I have to go give it to him. Can I go? Will they let me see him yet?"

"Let's go see!" Kanta said, and then added, "I am always so proud of you. I know you know it, but I don't always say it, and I want you to really know. I think you might be the only person that will be able to get through to your dad, to help him see the truth."

7

"Hello, can I speak to Allie Kramer?" a man's voice asked through the phone.

"Yes, this is she."

"Hello, Allie. My name is Harvey Akers. I got your number from Nani…"

Allie saved him from explaining any further. "Yes, of course. I know who you are."

"Okay, good," he spoke hesitantly, the shock and grief still clear in his voice.

He recounted the most recent details first, the ones of his wife's last weeks and how he found her. "She was only thirty-nine," he lamented. Then he went through the course of their courtship and subsequent marriage–they had just had their one-year anniversary before she died. He said that she was absolutely beautiful, and more importantly than that, an angel. He talked about how meeting her had saved him from the ravages of his tragic life. He talked about their love. She was the love of his life.

Allie hung up the phone in painful disbelief. She fought through the numbness in her hands to try to pick the phone back up to call Grace. But she wasn't ready yet. Her brained swirled with memories and projections into the future. What would she do? How could she possibly make up for her involvement in this? She was back in the same guttural shock as when Grace had told her the news about the "voluntary recall" of Senecox, except this time it was so much worse. This time instead of only imagining how this situation would be affecting people at the personal level, she had talked to a real person, a person with flesh and bones, a personality and a life story, and the worst of all, a love story. She was no longer wondering about the possible individual implications. She was hearing and feeling, over and over again in her mind, the grief, pain, and shock in the voice of Harvey Akers. The sadness and gut-wrenching loss he was experiencing at the premature departure of the soul that was his wife, the love of his life. She remembered how she sat through hours of "obstacle handling" meetings to successfully counter competitor claims that Senecox was killing people. "It is an absolute necessity to handle this obstacle," Centaury drilled into them, because market share depended on it. Market share? Even then she knew the stupidity of it all, but she was really convinced that Fester Pharmaceuticals, their main competitor in that market, was really evil. She would jokingly refer to them as "the devil incarnate". Why else would they lie, steal samples, spread untrue rumors about competitor reps, and exhibit the barrage of other incorrigible behaviors she dealt with daily? Could there have been some truth behind the mess of deception? As she sat watching the tide roll into the canal outside her window, she knew the answer to that question once and for all.

Allie reflected on the dictionary meaning of Centaur: a Greek mythological creature with the upper half of a man holding a bow and arrow, and the lower half of a horse. *Only half human fighting to survive at any cost, and half horse's ass is more like it,* she thought.

As the numbness wore off, it was replaced with the now familiar drive to action. Weakness turned to strength; paralysis shifted into a need for movement towards *something.* Her eyes squinted with burgeoning rage. She removed the phone from the receiver with purpose and dialed. Many miles away, a small, clean cell phone rang in a fabulous purse with perfectly matching shoes somewhere nearby. It was answered with the same deliberate intention as the caller carried when dialing. They knew it was time.

"Allie, I'm ready."

"Okay, Gracie, that's good, because it's time."

Allie filled her in on the conversation with Harvey Akers and her corresponding thoughts and emotions. It wasn't a coincidence that Grace was having the same pain, frustration, and helplessness with her situation.

"I'm going to write the book, Gracie. I have to. It's the only way. People have to know. They have to know; they have to see. The only way we can change anything is by helping educate people about reality. There is power in numbers."

"What about my situation? What do I do?" Gracie exclaimed, exasperation rolling off her into the receiver.

"We have to get pissed off and stay pissed off for right now. That will at least keep us out of the pits of despair and helplessness. Anger will keep us in action, and that is what it is going to take to make something happen."

"I can definitely do that," Gracie said, starting to think about the nonchalance and confidence with which her manager told her that she was going to break the law and there was nothing she could do about it.

Allie's thoughts drifted to Gracie's interaction with her manager. "Now, let's think a second here. The only way that guy could have enough certainty to act like that to you on that serious of a matter is because…"

Gracie interrupted with a smirk, "Is because he is an asshole!?"

"Yeah, that too," Allie concurred. "But also because he must know that the safety of the situation is so wired into the upper echelons of the company, the FDA, and the government that he felt invincible."

Invincible, Grace reflected. That was exactly how he acted. They were both quieted by the word. How could people doing wrong things really be invincible?

Allie focused again, so caught up in her brain that she was staring out the window without seeing anything. "All we have to prove is that the antibiotic companies, the FDA and the government, all had access to sufficient information to prove negligence. If there is data out there about antibiotic resistance and Superbug formation, which there obviously is, then there is a case against all of them. Most of the need for antibiotics in livestock comes from the living conditions of the animals and the unsanitary conditions of the farm. I believe there is a really solid case against the pharmaceutical companies that sell antibiotics for livestock, because they have to have been aware of the possible implications of their sale of the drugs. The case against the FDA is even stronger, because it is their job to protect the public and they have slacked not only in the area of the actual drugs, but in the allowance of pesticide use and continuation of unclean, unsafe living conditions for animals. The government is ultimately responsible for everything, because they are watching it all go on without intervening."

"So, what do I do now?" Gracie pleaded.

"Well, since we definitely know that I'm going to write the book, we have to get as much information on all of these topics as possible to disseminate through the book. We want people to be motivated to find their own truth. We want to give them enough information so that it will pique their interest enough to do their own research and create their own force in their individual spheres of influence, with all of us moving toward the same goals. So, I guess what we have to do now is gather information."

"Okay, I'm on it," Gracie said triumphantly.

"Me too," Allie sighed.

As they hung up, Allie's rage had softened. *Damn it,* she thought, *I did it again!* She realized that she had fallen back into fear and subsequent anger. She reminded herself that she didn't want to create from anger and fear anymore. She was intent on moving through this process as consciously and with as much love as possible. She reminded herself that even the companies of Big Pharma, the FDA, the government, and everything else, was made up of people, of individuals, who were working through their individual issues the same as she was. She was no better than them. Her lofty goals, good intentions, and newfound focus on her spiritual path did not stop her from becoming afraid and angry, certainly not because she had just fallen into it again without even realizing it. But that's okay, she consoled herself. She realized it now, and she was going to change the way she was looking at it. Instead of seeing this as a crusade of good against evil, she was going to try to remember that she was just playing her part in the restoration of the balance of things, and she was determined to do it from as much of a place of non-judgment as she possibly could. She also remembered that this was a process, her process, and everyone else's, and the outcome really didn't matter; it was how it was done and having consciousness during the doing.

9

MOTHER AND SON PULLED UP TO FRIEND'S HOSPITAL IN Philadelphia. The beautiful grounds took some of the creepiness of the place away, but there was still that hospital smell and the wretched coldness. Why were hospitals always so cold and how did they get that universal hospital smell? The attendant at the desk looked surprisingly colorful and chipper. She was wearing a bright pink blouse with big, gaudy-but-matching earrings. It was amazing how resilient humans could be. To be able to stay consistently composed in that environment was truly amazing and inspirational.

Kanta made a mental note of her name tag that read "Eleanor" so she could write a letter of appreciation to her superiors. Eleanor met the task of figuring out if Tanti was ready to be seen with cheerful alacrity. She gave them the room number and directions with a smile, and they were on their way.

Eli let his mom go in first and patiently waited outside the door. When it was his turn, he took a deep breath, picked his old knapsack up off the floor and swung it around his arm, and went in. It wasn't like other hospital rooms he had been in before.

His dad looked at him and tears welled up in his eyes. "I'm so sorry. I'm so ashamed. You have always been ahead of your time. I wish I would have been open to some of your wisdom. My life has been a waste and has caused the destruction of life and happiness. It is unforgivable that you have to see me like this. I have nothing to offer anybody."

"That is not true!" Eli gasped. "You may have nothing to offer from your current mental perspective, but if you change that perspective you could see your gifts."

"My gifts got me here. My gifts have hurt and killed people."

"Your gifts have also helped people and could help so many more. All it will take is a change in your view and a corresponding change in the direction of your path. You are one of the world's most brilliant research scientists. You got pulled into the American way. It's okay. You're not the only one. All of our culture is based on all of the things that you're getting down on yourself about. You could make up your mind to use your intelligence to change the system."

"It's impossible to change the system. Defense systems for keeping the system intact are inherent within it. You can't break that and neither can I. I've always told you this. That's why we just have to find a comfortable place, our place, inside the system."

"Are you listening to yourself? Can you hear yourself defending the system like it's your own defense system? That is because it *is* your own defense system. Remember that this is the order that you just said wasn't working for you. I know it's hard to see past all of this right now, but can you open up for just a second to something greater?"

Tanti nodded and Eli continued. "Now, I know that you've never really been interested in anything I've been studying, but I really feel like the things I figured out are really relevant to your getting out of here, coming home, and having a happy, productive life. There's so much, I don't even know where to start."

"It may as well be at the beginning. I'm sorry I've missed so much of your growth process because of my closed-mindedness. Will you get your mother so she can hear, too?"

Eli popped his head outside and his mother's face beamed back at him. "Can you come in?"

They filled her in on the prelude to what was coming and then Eli began, "Well, as you know, I have been disgusted and frustrated with the whole way things are done, specifically in this country, because that's what I'm most familiar with, but really it's been with mankind in general. My process started with my educating myself, which led to awareness of different facets of problems we are all faced with, then my natural progression was to try to fix it all. My first attempts at this were my websites. I thought if I educated people that would be the beginning of their process and then we could all be aware and motivated to fix things together. My studies went to the structure of government and social order. It then went to history to fill in more understanding about the aforementioned topics and to get more specifics on the evolution of health care specifically. Now, I'm summarizing these things in minutes, but each part represent months and years of my process. I then opened up to philosophy to try to get some guidance on building the perfect system, which then led to religion. But I just felt like I wasn't getting anywhere, like I was running around in circles. It wasn't until I opened up to God and asked for help that I really started to get somewhere.

"I studied myriad belief systems and put together charts highlighting their common threads. Now you can imagine there have been a lot of details within all of these systems, most of which are in this book bag. But it was as I compared the details of all of the different religious texts that I had the first big breakthrough–IT'S ALL THE SAME... ALL OF IT! There is only one God, and each of the prophets that headed each of the major religious movements were all speakers of the truth, the same truth, the one truth. On the quantum physics level this idea is supported, because down to the tiniest levels measurable it's all the same stuff. All of it. We are made out of the same things that created our galaxy and the other galaxies. Our bodies are made from the same thing this building is made of. Down at the very tiny molecular level is a shape called the flower of life, which is also synonymous with the idea of the Fibonacci Code, the same standard ratio that is in Leonardo Da Vinci's work, is the same ratio in every single thing! So, the separation we feel from God, the separation we feel from ourselves and from others, the separation of religions and people, is all an illusion. The idea that the Garden of Eden teaches about, how our Free Will, created separation, is the explanation of what happened. As soon as we got Free Will we were able to think that we were separate from God. But we're really not; we never were. And I believe that is what we are here to learn, or should I say, *remember*.

The next huge awareness I came to was that everything in our lives is a mirror for us; it shows us directly what our soul needs to learn to evolve. So, with that belief we are forced into non-judgment, because everything is really stuff our soul created to help us learn and everybody had to eventually learn all the same things. The wars in the world are reflections of the lack of peace inside each of us. Who do you know that really has peace inside? How could the world be anything but what *we* are?

"The government, which has been at the brunt of my, and everyone else's, judgment and frustration is really a mirror of our internal strife, and more specifically, the governmental system actually symbolizes our own egoic structure. The government more than symbolizes our own egoic structure; it is actually the physical incarnation of it, our mirror of it. It is there to show us that at our current level of consciousness we are incapable of governing ourselves, so we had to externalize that need. The same way our ego has defense mechanisms that keep it in place, like you said before, the government has the same mechanisms that keep it in place. The reason we haven't been able to make any changes in the system is because the general consciousness has stayed the same. We haven't gotten closer to getting beyond our own limiting factors because the focus has been on blaming outside forces ; outside forces that we actually created to show us what we need to work on. The need for police and the legal system has come because people haven't been able to control themselves, so they have externalized a system of enforcement, judgment, and punishment to keep them in line. However, when people really heal and get beyond their own ego system to the real oneness behind the veil, outside enforcement won't be necessary and people will be self-governed. As the general consciousness evolves, the need for all of these terrible external reflections of our inner problems will fall away on their own weight, because our new, evolved selves will be reflected out into the external world. It will only be by each individual being aware of this phenomena and being accountable for their creations that we will ever be able to change the world."

Tanti and Kanta were silent and listening very intently. Tanti was trying to find the words to ask the first of many questions about what Eli said.

"What you're saying is very interesting. I don't know that I'm really getting all of it yet. I'm having trouble relating this perspective to my particular situation."

"The first step to figuring that out is to describe how the situation makes you feel."

Tanti searched his brain for the right words. "I feel lost, disconnected."

"Well, if you apply this idea of the mirror, you feel disconnected from everything outside because you have lost your inner connection with your higher self, who you really are."

Tanti looked at his son mournfully and knew that it was true. "So, how do I get it back?"

Eli's insides bubbled up with excitement and he felt so light he was sure if he was standing on a scale it wouldn't even measure any weight. He grabbed his book bag and whisked out a hardcover book of moderate thickness with a glossy white paper cover that read, "The Marriage of Spirit - Enlightened Living in Today's World" by Leslie Temple-Thurston with Brad Laughlin.

"I'm going to leave this with you. I know it will answer most, if not all, of those unanswered questions."

Tanti extended his hand and took the book. His wrist bent with the unexpected weight of it on his frail hand. For the first time since he had gotten there, he felt a stirring of motivation to restore his health.

10

ALLIE AWOKE TO THE UNFAMILIAR SOUND OF A FAX COMING through. Her business activities these days were leisurely, on her own time, and never involved unsolicited faxes coming through. She jumped up and slid across the slick floor in her furry purple socks, almost running right into the fax machine. She giggled at how much she loved the socks, because they were soft and purple and didn't match a damn thing she had, but here she found another reason for them to be her favorite–their slide-ability. By the time she got to the machine, enough of the fax had printed for her to understand the early-morning urgency. It read: "U.S. Food and Drug Administration–FDA consumer–September/October 1999–CAMPYLOBACTER–LOW-PROFILE BUG IS FOOD POISONING LEADER." She smiled at the immediacy and quality of Gracie's research. Her eyes speed-read through the fax. She noted an area that talked about increased susceptibility of children, elderly, and sick people. She marked it. This was, of course, a big argument in their favor. Chickens, like people, were more susceptible to this and other microbes when their immune systems weren't functioning at a moderate or high level. With the way poultry was raised and kept, they had everything going against their optimal immune system function.

Her eyes fell on point number two to be marked: "In addition, with the emergence of antibiotic-resistant Campylobacter, 'the true magnitude of the problem is becoming clearer,' says Angulo, who also heads the Center for Disease Control arm of the National Antimicrobial Resistance Monitoring System." Her eyes scrolled down the page resting on point number three: "CDC studies also show an increase in resistance to fluoroquinolones and this can be correlated to fluoroquinolone use in poultry, according to Angulo. In addition, "We did a case control study in 1997, comparing people with non-resistant Campylobacter infections with fluoroquinolone-resistant infections, and found that those with resistant infections were more likely to have severe infections, bloody diarrhea, and be hospitalized... Because of the concern over antibiotic resistance, the FDA is considering whether, before it reviews a new animal drug for approval, manufacturers must assess the likelihood that use of a certain drug in food animals will transfer resistance and create a public health problem. In addition, new procedures for monitoring antibiotic use and resistance after approval also are being considered. 'FDA believes a new regulatory framework is needed to address resistance concerns raised by the food-animal use of antibiotics,' says Goodman, who also serves as a Deputy Medical Director for FDA."

So, there's the proof then! They did know and as of yet, they've done nothing! It continued, "Hollinger says, 'At this time we are not taking action toward withdrawal of these products from the market. We have asked the sponsors of poultry fluoroquinolone products to provide data that would describe the prevalence of resistance in poultry flocks and identify possible actions to prevent the emergence of disease in treated flocks.' " A lot of good *that* will do if they are all in cahoots! They already know about the problem!

She read on with growing aversion, "'Link to Guillain-Barré–Campylobacter is not the only thing that triggers Guillain-Barré syndrome, but it is now recognized as one of the disorder's major forerunners. Guillain-Barré, which also may follow a viral illness, is an autoimmune attack on the peripheral nerves that can cause weakness and paralysis. Annually, about two people per 100,000 contract the syndrome. We also know that many patients who have campylobacteriosis seem to have a more severe form of Guillain-Barré,' Leshner says."

God! she thought, *what do they need to know to stop this?! It seems like according to their own website, they already know more than enough!* She caught herself getting angry again and reminded herself that when she has a reaction to anything, it is her own feelings inside that are to be dealt with. She was convinced that she could do her part without getting caught up the judgment-guilt-shame cycle. After all, cultivating that ability was really the point.

11

ON THIS SUNNY MORNING, TANTI TUNTASIT WAS SO grateful for the choice of hospitals that his wife made on such short notice. He had refused to leave his room until this morning. He told his nurse that he would like to go outside to read his book. It was then that she informed him that Friend's Hospital had a one-hundred-acre campus full of horticultural wizardry. There was actually a "horticultural therapy" program that was instituted by the hospital to help patients heal and deal with stress through the joys of gardening. She said to let him know if he wanted to partake in the program at any point. He graciously accepted the information and promised he would think about it. Today, though, his focus was the book. As she rolled him down into the gardens, he saw other patients taking part in everything from leisurely gardening activities to vegetative restfulness. He was somewhere in the middle, like a balance between the two, a feeling that he came to see as strangely coincidental as he progressed through the book.

The author wrote of the unification of opposites through spiritual and mental exercises, and the subsequent ability to rise above either extreme to find the true divine balance that is above the dualities of the planet. Her story started out as one of a "reluctant mystic". It seemed when everybody fell into their spirituality, it came as a result of not being able to deny the "knowing" anymore. Tanti, too, had felt it start to sprinkle over him on several occasions throughout his life, including the birth of his son. As he watched the miracle, he knew, he just *knew*, that there had to be something greater, something higher, than the life that he knew, that everybody knew. But his logical brain was so well-versed at squashing these little feelings as they would start to arise, that they never really got very far. "You're a scientist! The only things that are real are the ones that can be proven in a lab." There was no room for all of this spiritual stuff when there was billions of dollars on the line.

He looked around the gardens and he felt a little sadness take over him when he realized that *he* had created this. He hadn't listened to any of his muffled and muted better judgment, and now it had come to this. The life that he had was so entrenched in fear that he had missed out on really living. Before he sank too low he smiled, remembering that there was not only still hope, but that he could put the living back in his life, and he was the only one that could do it. He was accountable. He reveled in the burden and the promise of his discovery. He made this mess, and he could fix it, and this book was going to show him how. Ultimately, he had to break down his own defense system, his egoic structure, through a process the book called "processing". It was believed that using the exercises one could do ten years worth of healing in two years.

It was the ego that made us feel separate, he read, but there was wholeness and unification behind the illusion of separation. By breaking down the ego, one could return to the wholeness that one never really left. "THE PERSONALITY IS FALSE IDENTIFICATION. What stops us from knowing our own enlightenment is our identification with the conditioned personality," he read in a whisper. After all, he thought, what was the self that he knew but a compilation of the different personality matrices that he had accumulated over his lifetime? Every time he played a role to somebody, that role got added to the matrix list. He was a son, a brother, a husband, an employee, a taxpayer, a father, and so much more, and each role had added to the amount of his selves, because he unconsciously played his parts without looking any further into himself. To get at his real self, he had to wade through this soup of pretend selves. Then he could be even better at the normal roles he had to play in life, because he would be living in awareness and truth. He felt ready to start the exercises that would help him remember who he really was.

He pulled out the five-subject notebook that Eli had given him along with the book. He remembered his son's face as he handed it to him. "Here, you'll need this, too," he said, peering out of small dark eyes over the top of the book, which he held with both hands as he passed it. He spread both books out on the concrete table before him. He was alone in the shady alcove. The wind was cool on his thin skin, but it was unseasonably warm for an autumn day in Philadelphia.

The book read that if one were ready to start the exercises, they would then skip to section two, page 142. There was a quote by Shankara with a beautiful mandala above it. He didn't know who Shankara was, but took in the essence of his words just the same: "I dwell within; I am without. I am before and behind, I am in the south and I am in the north. I am above and I am below. The wave, the foam, the eddy, and the bubble are all essentially water. Similarly, the body and ego are really nothing but pure consciousness. Everything is essentially consciousness, purity, and joy."

Section two began, "The 'unification of opposite's' techniques are mental tools to help us unravel the knots of the mind. They offer a very fast way to balance our lives and wake up, and were given for this particularly accelerated time we are living in. They are age-old principles, truths from the ancient mystery schools and traditions, and have been revamped and streamlined for the modern era."

The first exercise was called "Polarities". It was a seven-step process. The author said to make sure one had uninterrupted time to work on each exercise. He smiled, knowing that he had nothing but time.

Step one: Pick an experience that carried some kind of emotional charge. It could be an old, childhood occurrence, or a very recent experience.

Step two: Write about the experience. Write the story as you felt it happen. No punctuation or correct spelling was needed. Use as many descriptive words to capture the thoughts, emotions, and states of mind involved.

Step three: Pick out the theme words and phrases which have a charge for you.

Step four: Make a list of the theme words and phrases in a single column down the left side of the page. You can add any additional words or phrases that come to your mind while writing the list.

Step five: Find the opposites and write them in the right column next to each word.

Step six: Offer it up with a prayer (example: Oh Eternity, please take all of these states of mind which are unbalanced in this pattern and balance and clear them. Do this so that I may see more clearly and find my way home more easily. I give thanks knowing it will be done. I offer this up and wait for Grace).

Step seven: Wait for Grace. Go for a walk or have something to eat, or just sit. When Grace comes in, you may feel it right away or all of a sudden you feel better and lighter, and can't remember when it actually clicked.

Tanti clicked open his pen. He began writing about the day that he heard about the recall:

"I was sorting mail in my office, and was just about to go into the lab when a loud beep sounded followed by a voice asking all employees to come to the meeting room immediately. The voice was a familiar one, it was my beloved superior, whom I trust and respect. I grabbed my lab jacket and felt a plunging in my stomach. It didn't sound good and I was really nervous. I hurried into the meeting room where all of my counterparts were already sitting. My boss and counterpart thanked us for coming, and said, 'Please know that this is the hardest thing I have ever had to do. The compound we know as MC-457, that was discovered right here in this laboratory, has been pulled off the market. It was voluntary, but it would have been forced if we didn't do it.' The details of what else he said doesn't matter, but the feelings that everyone shared, but especially felt by me, were overwhelming. He had spared me from mentioning it, but it was I who discovered the compound. The guilt and shame convulsed in me and I could taste bile coming up into my mouth. The disgrace was too much to handle. I felt like the weight of loss of life, broken families, and prematurely-ended dreams were all on my shoulders. The guilt...."

Tanti couldn't write anymore, and didn't really write much, but somehow just writing it down was such a tremendous relief to him. He moved to step three, circling the themes and catch phrases that carried a charge for him. He wrote the column of words and phrases, and began to work on the opposites. This was the first time in this new process that he hesitated. He realized it was, because it was now that he was trying to access the things that had remained unconscious. For every feeling and thought that was conscious, its opposite counterpart was lurking somewhere, sometimes readily accessible, sometimes hidden, buried. It was those buried things that were creating. Eighty-ninety percent of the brain's capacity is in its unconsciousness. We create from our brains. So, most of what we created, we weren't even aware of as being inside of us. "Guilt, guilt," he racked his brain. "What was the opposite of guilt?"

He twisted and contorted his brain looking for the best word. It seemed like there were more than a few words, but the best one was freedom. If he didn't have to feel guilty, he would feel free. That was it: Free! The book said that as he figured out his own puzzle, he would start unlocking and he felt this. He really felt it! The words could be different for each person, but that was what it was all about, the individual unlocking themselves, freeing themselves from the ties that bound them up in knots. He moved through the opposites work and when he finished, he said his prayer and offered it up to Grace. It was about that time that he was ready for dinner. He hadn't really been eating, but now, all of a sudden, he was so voracious for sustenance, for anything that would boost his life force. He felt very strange. He was trying to figure out the word to describe the way he felt. Then, his face beamed and he smiled ear to ear when he realized what it was. He felt alive!

12

ALLIE SAT AT HER DESK. FINALLY, IT WAS TIME TO OPEN THE windows! Everyone in Florida suffered through the six months of summer heat madness, and at the end of October it all became worth it. The breeze massaged her face with life. She took another look at the fax. It was really crazy. Campylobacter was just *one* microbe, and it had so many ill effects. She recalled again how Centaury would always tout a low percentage of side effects. She would always think in terms of the individual. If sixty-eight percent of people had such-and-such a side effect, and one million people took the drug, then around seventy thousand people would be having the side effect! So seventy thousand individuals would be experiencing the actual side effect, and God knows how many more family members and friends were adjusting their lives to deal with it. Then, of course, there's the cost for dealing with that side effect through other treatments or medications. It didn't make any sense.

Anyway, if all of those people were affected by one microbe, the liability for the rest of the microbes would be astronomical. She wasn't fond of lawsuits as a way to deal with things unless it was absolutely well grounded and necessary, but it was looking like that might be just the thing that was needed. If every person effected personally, or that had lost a family member on account of the inability of the FDA and all levels of government to clean up the agriculture and pharmaceutical industry, filed negligence suits against them, then it would certainly send a wake up call. It wouldn't be safe to partake in cronyism or voting based on financial kickbacks, and *that* would make it all worthwhile.

Now, she wasn't even considering taking the lawsuit thing on herself, but she knew that she didn't have to. If the information got to the right people, then it would all flow from there. Just imagine it, she thought, a class-action lawsuit against the FDA!

13

GRACE WAS DOWNRIGHT DANGEROUS WHEN SHE GOT focused on something. Fire blazed out of her eyes as she poured over books, magazines, and papers she'd printed off of the Internet. As she read over the material, she found so many unthinkable things that the government was involved in that she became overwhelmed. Somewhere in the mess of literature were the plans for a car engine that functioned just on seawater and its only by-product was regular water. All this information coming out during a time when we were fighting a war for oil! There was information about chemical trails distributed by the government via airplanes in certain parts of the country. There was a separate pile just on top-secret information the government had relating to UFO's. But the sheets she laid her fiery eyes on now were specific to the farming industry. She had always known that the farmers get the crappy end of the stick in so many ways, and this lot was ensured for them by the big meat companies. It was really the meat companies that her company sold to, but for some reason they had the sales force at the farms. She was realizing just at that moment that this was part of the whole charade. Making it seem like anyone other than the big companies had any choices was just part of the game. Allie must have been playing in that sandbox, too. It was really the big government contracts for the pharmaceutical drugs for places like the veterans hospitals that made the big dents in market share, and consequently the bottom line dollar figures. They were all pawns in a pathetic fixed chess game.

The meat companies needed as much meat produced in the shortest amount of time in order to keep increasing sales. Mom and Pop farms either played by their rules or were forced under. It is because of them that farming practices which were more in sync with the land were pushed aside. They then convinced farmers that they couldn't make it without the contracts from the meat companies, and most were forced to surrender. The best thing that could be done, she decided, was for everyone to buy organic meat to show support for the organic farmers. But how would she let everyone know? The little more that organic items cost helped to support a life and community, and a world of getting back to basics. Maybe Allie could include that in the book?

She pulled herself back to her project and ignored the ticking clock passing 2:00 a.m.

14

WHEN ELI WENT BACK TO SEE HIS DAD, HE ALMOST FELL down at the sight of him. His color had returned and his protruding bones had begun to have a soft cover of flesh. *How long has it been?* he thought. It couldn't have been more than a few days.

Tanti greeted him with a hug that was so strong it borderedlined a wrestling move Eli had seen once on the television.

He motioned for his son to sit down, brought out his notebook, and started leafing through the many pages he had 'processed' since Eli was last there.

Eli gasped with surprise and delight. He could see the future unfolding before his eyes, and he thought of Mama and how she would always just *know* things. All of a sudden, he understood. Now he could see it, too. He knew that he and his dad would teach classes based on this 'beloved book' as he called it. He knew that all of his computer skills and his dad's scientific skills would somehow play into the plan. The plan....

His thoughts went again to Mama. He hadn't seen her in so long because of everything that was going on. He started to get a little nervous thinking he needed to tell her, but then he could see her, as always, leaning over with one hand on her big thigh and one hand holding a finger up to her mouth. "Shh, Mama knows..." No doubt she knew, and he laughed a little thinking that she probably knew even before him.

When he left, he went to go see her on her bench, the same bench where she had been for all these years, but the bench was empty–she was gone. As he walked through the park, autumn swirling around him, he wondered if she was ever really there.

15

ALLIE THOUGHT OF THE MAGNITUDE OF THE SITUATION AT hand. Orchestrating change on this level was such a big deal and had implications she could never imagine. She started to feel uncomfortable. She recognized the discomfort not only as fear of the outcomes, but more because of this expanding idea of spiritual integrity. It was the same way as she thought when she got the job with Centaury, that all of her youth, fire, and talent was being used for the best possible missions, later realizing that the time was not well-placed. She felt this about her new path. When she felt angry, she wanted to hold the government, the FDA, and any and all individuals involved in the quagmire, responsible. She felt the need to use her energy to ensure that outcome. She remembered that she didn't want to create from anger or fear anymore. It was such a tough habit to break! At this point, she really believed in the need for each person, including herself, to be accountable for their portion of the mess that was being reflected back. Spending her time pushing a lawsuit of monumental proportion wasn't focusing on self-accountability and therefore, wasn't teaching self-accountability, which is what, at this point, she believed was the most important message she could spread.

She thought about the day that she was ordained as a minister. She was a Minister of the Truth, the One Truth, and her life was her ministry. Anyone whose teachings were any consequence over the course of history taught by example, example of how they lived. She decided that in order to follow her highest path, she needed to do the same.

She knew what she had to do. She reached for her phone, reluctantly at first, but with the force of her decision gathering momentum, she dialed.

16

GRACIE'S SMALL WELL-MANICURED HAND PICKED UP THE
phone with excitement. She was ready to share all of her
research with Allie and reached for her pile of papers. In
a few seconds, she dropped the thick pile back on the
table accompanied by the worst kind of sourpuss face anyone could ever imagine.

"What do you mean? What are you talking about?"
she protested, standing up and clomping around in her
black slippers.

"How am I accountable for what these assholes who
call themselves humans have done? Have you gone crazy?
How do I have anything to do with what these demons
parading around in human bodies are doing? I am the vic-
tim here," Grace spouted out, sounding defeated.

Allie paused for a moment, silently asking the universe for the perfect words. "If you believe that there is
something more than just this human experience that we
are having, which I know you do, and if you believe that
we are souls having a human experience, then also
remember that we picked this experience. We each picked
our particular experience so that we could grow our soul

back to our highest source. We came into this existence alone and we leave alone. Our path here is about us, about our spirit's growth. Every person and situation is a mirror for us of what we have to heal. Remember what Jesus said, 'Judge not lest ye be judged. He without sin cast the first stone.' We have been going about this whole thing from a place of judgment, not from a place of love and compassion. If we truly know that in some lifetime we were all of the things that we hate in this lifetime, we have become more enlightened. If we choose the path that uses these external things to grow our soul, then we are on the true path of enlightenment."

Grace softened slightly. She thought of Jesus. He did definitely teach the principles of compassion, non-judgment, and unconditional love, and most people did definitely sway from that understanding with their thoughts and actions.

She took a deep breath and said, "Okay, I hear you."

Part VI

1

As Grace Avila knelt down in the pew, she stared up at the cross. She was still trying to understand what it all meant, but she was sure of one thing. Jesus taught unconditional love and forgiveness, and like Allie had reminded her years before, you can't be in anger or fear and love at the same time. So, what she did know was that any decisions or actions made from a place of anger weren't the highest choices, and couldn't possibly have the highest outcomes.

She got up and folded up the place where she had just knelt. She was the only one in there, and the sound of her soft pink heels resounded off of the wood floors and bounced around the empty church. She smoothed down the bunches in her pink wool, tea-length skirt as she gazed up at the stained glass windows over the door to the outside. Before she pushed the gold metal bar to release the door, she looked back at the cross. She swore that the face on the cross had changed to a smile, and she grimaced in surprise. She shook her head as if to try to forget, and stepped out into the cool autumn air. The man on the cross behind her was still smiling as the door squeaked closed in front of him.

Grace got into her car feeling light and free. She drove to the restaurant where she was meeting her manager for lunch. As she pulled up to the small diner, she glanced at herself in the rearview mirror. Bright emerald eyes shone back at her and she felt like she looked different, better, happier. She walked into the diner and spotted the man she was meeting; the man, until very, very recently, she detested with such vigor that she almost had to grow a second liver to make all the bile that she tasted in her mouth whenever she thought of him. But now she saw only light around him. It was truly a miracle. She slid into the bench with the grace and strength of a changed woman. She looked into the eyes of her former nemesis and she noticed that her former "I hope you rot in Hell smile" had grown into a genuine smile of compassion. While he was quite arrogant and self-assured in her past interactions with him, he grew uncomfortable with her energy change and shifted in his seat like a fidgety kindergartener.

She would have done anything to elicit this discomfort in him in the past, but now she barely noticed. She handed him her resignation letter and told him that she had decided "to pursue other opportunities". She was in too good of a positive place to recognize the irony of this statement. The big companies were always throwing canned answers at their sales people and now she threw the same typical canned answer back at him. Deciding to pursue other opportunities was the standard reason people gave for leaving a job they hate to do something that they feel really matters.

She walked away from the meeting with a spring in her step and the whole world open to her. She was going to write children's books. She was going to help mold and heal their minds before they turned into hardened, angry adults. She would leave helping the hardened, angry adults to Allie.

2

ELI WALKED THROUGH THE GARDENS AT FRIEND'S HOSPITAL on the way to see his father. For the first time in a long time, his father wasn't a patient. He rounded the curve and found his dear father standing in front of a table where ten patients of different ages were sitting. Eli smiled as he saw the ten five-subject notebooks open to blank pages. His father looked up at him and winked. Eli smiled with gratitude and understanding as he waved and walked away. He had wanted to tell his dad about his new website, a website based in faith–ConsciousnessIsConta-gious.com

3

It was time. Allie opened up to where she had started writing so many years ago and skipped a page. As soon as she picked up the pen, the perfect words came pouring out. She wrote:

November 1998

"He could tell by the unbridled excitement she was suppressing with a contorted face that she must have gotten the job: the job of a lifetime; the job she had done so well in school to get; the one she had researched and hunted for since before he knew her. It made her sacrifices all worthwhile. She was there."

Printed in the United States
113582LV00001B/7-18/A